Aristocrats, Plebeians and Revolution in England 1640–1660

A Socialist History of Britain

Series edited by the Northern Marxist Historians Group

Also available

John Newsinger, *Fenianism in Mid-Victorian Britain*

John Saville, *The Consolidation of the Capitalist State, 1800–1850*

Aristocrats, Plebeians and Revolution in England 1640–1660

Brian Manning

Pluto Press

LONDON · EAST HAVEN, CT

First published 1996 by Pluto Press
345 Archway Road, London N6 5AA
and 140 Commerce Street,
East Haven, Connecticut 06512, USA

British Library Cataloguing in Publication Data
A catalogue record for his book is available from the British
Library

ISBN 0 7453 0940 2

Library of Congress Cataloging in Publication Data
Manning, Brian
  Aristocrats, plebeians, and revolution in England, 1640–1660/
Brian Manning
     p.   cm. — (A Socialist history of Britain)
  Includes bibliographical references.
  ISBN 0–7453–0940–2 (hc)
  1. Great Britain — History — Puritan Revolution,
1640–1660. 2. Aristocracy (Social class) — England — History
— 17th century. 3. Social conflict — England — History–17th
century. 4. Working class — England — History — 17th
century. I. Title. II. Series.
DA405.M358 1996
941.06'2—dc20   95–38686
                                                            CIP

Designed and produced for Pluto Press by
Chase Production Services, Chipping Norton, OX7 5QR
Typeset from disk by Stanford DTP Services, Milton Keynes
Printed in the EC by WSOY, Finland

Contents

Acknowledgement

I am grateful to Norah Carlin, Christopher Hill, Ann Hughes, John Morrill, and John Rees for the great pains they took (and perhaps suffered) in reading my first draft of this book, and for discussions with Andy Wood. Their comments have led to many improvements in my final version, and have been especially stimulating as coming from different interpretations of the revolution, nevertheless my exposition will not end these differences.

Summary of Events

1625		Charles I succeeds to the throne.
1629		He dissolves his third parliament and rules for the next eleven years without summoning another (the 'Personal Rule').
1633		William Laud appointed Archbishop of Canterbury.
1634		Levying of 'Shipmoney' begins.
1637		Prynne, Burton and Bastwick tried in the Court of Star Chamber.
1638		Imposition of a new prayer-book leads to rebellion in Scotland.
1640	13 April	Parliament meets.
	5 May	Parliament dissolved (the 'Short Parliament').
	11 May	Riot in London against Laud.
	June–July	Disorders amongst English soldiers conscripted to suppress the rebellion in Scotland.
	August	Scottish army invades England and occupies Northumberland and Durham.
	24 September	Great Council of the Peers meets at York.
	3 November	'Long Parliament' assembles.
	November–December	Demonstrations in support of Prynne, Burton and Bastwick.
	November–December	Earl of Strafford and Archbishop Laud impeached by the House of Commons.
	11 December	London petition for the abolition of episcopacy.
1641	16 February	Act passed for Triennial Parliaments.
	3–4 May	Demonstrations against Strafford.
	12 May	Strafford executed.
	5 July	Court of Star Chamber abolished.
	October	Rising in Ireland.
	27–29 December	Riots in London against bishops.

1642	4 January	King charges five leaders of the House of Commons with treason and tries to arrest them in parliament.
	10 January	Popular demonstrations in support of the Five Members cause the king to flee from London.
	19 June	King rejects the demands of the two Houses of Parliament contained in the Nineteen Propositions.
	July–August	The king and the two Houses each fears the other intends to resort to force and so both take to arms.
	22–25 August	Riots in Essex and Suffolk.
	23 October	Battle of Edgehill is indecisive but advantage passes to the king.
1643–44		Scots intervene in the English Civil War on the side of parliament.
1645	March–September	Risings of the 'clubmen' against the war.
	April	Parliament changes the commanders of its forces and forms the 'New Model Army'.
	14 June	Battle of Naseby: decisive victory for parliament.
1646		Royalists surrender.
	9 October	Episcopacy abolished.
1647	April–June	Soldiers of the New Model elect 'agitators' and refuse to disband until their grievances and the liberties of England settled.
	July	Demonstrations in London against the New Model: apprentices occupy parliament.
	August	New Model occupies London.
	October–November	Representatives of private soldiers and officers debate the settlement of the issues raised by the Civil War (the 'Putney Debates'), including the new constitution proposed by the Levellers as the 'Agreement of the People'.

1648	March–August	Second Civil War, in which Scots ally with the king, invade England and defeated at Battle of Preston on 17 August.
	September–December	Parliament negotiates for a settlement with the king.
	11 September	Levellers petition against parliament's proposed settlement and against the powers of the king and the House of Lords over legislation.
	2–6 December	New Model occupies London and purges parliament ('Pride's Purge') in order to prevent proposed settlement with king.
1649	20–27 January	King tried and sentenced to death.
	30 January	King executed.
	6–7 February	Monarchy and House of Lords abolished.
	28 March	Leveller leaders arrested and imprisoned.
	15 August	New Model begins conquest of Ireland.
1650	22 July	New Model begins conquest of Scotland.
1653	20 April	Cromwell dissolves the purged parliament (the 'Rump Parliament').
	16 December	Cromwell installed as Lord Protector.
1655		Jamaica captured by English expedition.
1658	3 September	Cromwell dies: his son Richard becomes Lord Protector.
1659	April–May	Army overthrows Richard and reinstates the 'Rump Parliament'.
	13 October	Army expels 'Rump Parliament'.
	5 December	Riot in London against the army.
	26 December	'Rump Parliament' restored as result of movement of soldiers and civilians against army leaders.
1660	21 February	Purged members re-admitted to parliament.
	16 March	Parliament dissolves itself.
	April–May	A new parliament elected (the 'Convention Parliament') and King Charles II recalled to the throne.

Introduction: The People and Revolution

For really I think that the poorest he that is in England has a
life to live, as the greatest he ...

COLONEL THOMAS RAINBOROUGH, 1647

Traditionally the events in England in the middle of the seventeenth
century – collapse of government, civil war and revolution – have
been seen as arising from divisions within the ruling class. Although
true up to a point, this does not justify historians studying only the
nobility and gentry, and perhaps the clergy, lawyers and merchants,
to explain these events. A vast amount of research has been devoted
to discovering the causes of the divisions amongst the nobility and
gentry, and the characteristics of those who took different sides,
as if the other 97 per cent of the population did not exist or did
not matter. More recently it has been recognised that people other
than lords and squires did play parts worthy of investigation – for
one thing they did most of the fighting and dying – and they did
not always follow blindly the lead of their social superiors.

Local history has been the most fertile and penetrating approach
to this period. Once beyond the study of counties in which gentry
appeared to be the only inhabitants, reaching out to regions, towns,
parishes, villages and neighbourhoods, it brought the people as a
whole into view, the diversity of their situations and their concerns,
disputes and struggles. Deference to their social superiors had
been bred into them, but was eroded by the events of 1640–60;
submission to landlords and employers who controlled their livelihoods was natural, but not to landlords and employers who took
away their livelihoods. They might follow their landlord or employer
into one of the parties in the Civil War, and they might learn of
politics and religion from their masters and ministers, but they were
not automatons. They had their own concerns and their own ideas.
Great issues were at stake for them as well as for the nobility and
gentry – their security, their livelihood, their welfare, their religion,
their customs and traditions and way of life; how to manage their
own small community and its relations with the world outside; how
to survive or how to prosper. These considerations might lead
them into one party or the other, or neither, and their reasons are

not less worthy of investigation than those of lords and squires, although more difficult because there is less evidence.

Popular movements do not, at any one time, necessarily involve many or most of the people, but are so termed here because they spring from amongst the people, from amongst those who are ruled rather than those who rule. They may embrace small or large numbers of active participants, although with many more passive sympathisers, and they may be radical or conservative, which in turn requires explanation. Radical is defined here as seeking the abolition or replacement rather than the reform of institutions. The breakdown of ecclesiastical control and the censorship gave the people, including the young and women, unprecedented opportunities to express themselves, and the weakening of control by the ruling class and of the state's means of coercion gave them opportunities to petition and to demonstrate. Freedom of speech, freedom of the press and freedom to demonstrate are the foundations of popular movements. Questions arose about how the people could defend themselves against exploitation by landlords and employers, and how they could take control of their own lives and their own society. They valued parliament – even though most of them were not represented in it – and the jury system; they valued the right to hold meetings and the right to make their views known to those in authority, and they often aspired to a more egalitarian society, sometimes even to a redistribution of wealth. When their rulers would not hear them, they took direct action.

J.H. Elliott sees three types of revolt in early modern Europe – aristocratic or popular, or a combination of the two. The threat of popular revolt, he says, was always present because of the pressure of population on food resources and the occurrence of harvest failure and starvation. As a result 'the possibility of popular uprisings was built into every society, and only a sudden tax increase or a rise in the price of bread was needed to precipitate a tumult. ... Mass insurrections born of hunger and misery' often acquired 'religious and millenarian overtones' and sometimes escalated into 'a violent protest against the whole ordering of society' (Elliott 1970: 110–2). Buchanan Sharp also attributes popular revolts to economic factors, 'such as inflation, unemployment, food scarcity, and enclosure', and observes that such revolts may become 'anti-aristocratic' when they were 'the result of social and economic grievances of such intensity that they took expression in violent outbreaks of what can only be called class hatred for the wealthy. Traditionally, such outbreaks took place in times of economic and social dislocation severe enough to free discontents from deferential controls', and the ruling class was blamed 'for the prevailing economic and social conditions' (Sharp 1980: 264–6). It is, however, too simple to reduce all popular revolts to automatic responses to economic stimuli. During the English Revolution economic distress did play a part in popular movements, and there was discontent at various points over unemployment, enclosures, increased bread prices or higher taxes, but there was no mass insurrection 'born of hunger and misery'. Economic distress led to rioting, but that did not challenge the ruling order. It was when popular movements became politicised, as many did during the revolution, that control by the ruling class could be threatened.

J.H. Elliott and Buchanan Sharp explore the relationships between popular and aristocratic revolts. Elliott suggests that either sort of revolt 'may provide conditions conducive to the outbreak of the other'. Popular revolt may furnish a section of the aristocracy with the occasion and the means to coerce the government or to take power from a rival faction of the aristocracy; or divisions within the aristocracy may create the opportunity for popular revolt: all these occurred in the breaking out of the English Revolution. Elliott further argues that a popular revolt only stood some chance of success if the governing class 'failed to rally to the crown and the agents of royal authority', or a section of the governing class actively participated in the revolt: the former was the case in England in 1640 and the latter in 1642 (Elliott 1970: 110–2). Buchanan Sharp distinguishes two types of revolt under aristocratic leadership, one being when the rank-and-file shared the reasons and objectives of the leaders, and the other being when 'the aims and motives of the rank-and-file were not those of the leaders'. In the latter type 'two different processes occurred in establishing aristocratic leadership':

> In one case, the disaffected common people would compel reluctant gentry to take leadership and thus give organisation and a measure of legitimisation to the movement ... In the other case, the leader's ability to attract a large following was merely fortuitous, that is, the discontents of the common people needed only a leader or an issue to set off a rebellion. The leaders, acting as igniters, often attracted a following out of all proportion to the cause they represented. It may be surmised, then, that the rank and file projected their cause onto the leader. (Sharp 1980: 264–6.)

This second case is applicable to the English Revolution. While it is true that the people often felt a need for aristocratic leadership, nevertheless it is demonstrable again and again, as Christopher Hill points out, that the people were capable of throwing up leaders from their own ranks. When aristocratic leaders detected that the aims and motives of their followers were not the same as their own, they withdrew and realigned themselves with the forces of order, and when the rank-and-file recognised that their cause differed from that of their aristocratic leaders, they turned to other leaders (Hill 1970: 205–6).

The problem with applying these analyses to the English Revolution is that they miss the essential element that made the situation in England different, and that was the presence of a substantial middle rank in the population between the wealthy aristocrats and the impoverished masses, and the role of these 'middle sort of people', as contemporaries termed them, in the revolution. While Norah Carlin is right to note that too much stress on the 'middle sort' can lead to ignoring or underplaying the involvement of the poorer peasants and artisans, as well as the wage labourers, in the revolution (Carlin 1980–81), there is also a danger of accepting a simple analysis in terms of a society polarised between rich and poor. Jonathan Barry points out that the excision by conservative historiography of the middle class from early modern society and the attack on the Marxist conception of bourgeois revolution, has led recent socialist historiography to adopt 'a polarized view of society (patrician and plebeian, for example)', and to see the 'conflict of interests in society as lying between elite and people ...' (Barry 1994). Thus it becomes necessary to put back the 'middle sort' into the English Revolution, while agreeing that it is not identical with the modern term 'middle class', and at the same time to locate this group both in leadership of broad popular movements and in conflicts of interest with the poor.

It is further necessary to restate that the revolution took place in a society being reshaped by the development of capitalism and the genesis of the modern middle and working classes. Without the factor of growing capitalism the dynamic of the revolution and its legacy is not fully explained. But the relationship between capitalism and the revolution is not a simple one of cause and effect, rather it is a correlation of economic and social trends with political and religious conflicts.

It is a false dichotomy in conservative historiography to set an interpretation in terms of religion against one in terms of class, and to regard religious explanation of the conflict as an alternative to social explanation. While it is clear that religious issues were very important, they do not explain everything, for religious conflicts coexisted with political, social and economic conflicts, and each influenced the other. Where consciousness of class differences emerged from the economic and social situation in which people found themselves, and their relations to the system of production, it shaped religious and political conflicts. It was not a society without class and class consciousness, as conservative historiography maintains: the class consciousness of the aristocracy can scarcely be doubted, but in the rest of the population class consciousness was less universal and more intermittent. Grievances or suffering evoked class feeling in localities where there were conflicts between peasant producers and their landlords, or of landless artisans and labourers with their employers, but such feeling was not usually projected onto national politics. The national political crisis, however, did evoke class consciousness in the radicalised sections of the 'middle sort'.

Popular movements played a part, perhaps a decisive part, in the revolution. This book views the actions of monarchs, aristocrats and generals in the context of society at large, and the contribution of the people to making history. Divisions amongst the people and their actions were at least as important as divisions amongst the aristocrats and their actions. Focus will be upon the crucial ingredient provided by the 'middle sort of people', but they could not control events on their own and had to attach themselves to a section of the aristocracy or to mobilise wider popular support.

This book does not provide a continuous narrative, and passes over the battles of the Civil War, but proceeds through a series of interlinked episodes to highlight selected themes: the precipitation of the fall of Charles I's government by popular resistance in 1640; the attempt of the aristocrats to take control; the split in the aristocracy in response to popular intervention in politics; the role of popular movements in the genesis of parties in the Civil War, but also the efforts of ordinary people to stop the war; the formative role of the radicalised sections of the 'middle sort of people' in the parliamentarian party; the rise of anti-aristocratic feeling; the influence of radical movements, notably the Levellers, after the Civil War; the emergence of a revolutionary army (the New Model Army) and its seizure of control in 1648–49, and the displacement of the aristocracy from political power. Finally, the analysis passes from the climax of the revolution in 1649 to the end of the revolution in 1658–60: the failure of the renewal of left-wing activity, the popular revolt against military rule and for parliamentary forms, and the regaining of political power by the aristocracy. As popular movements ushered in the revolution, so they ushered it out, but the world of 1660 was not the same as 1640.

CHAPTER 1

Society on the Eve of Revolution

'It has been the method of former times' that the peers and gentry in parliament 'consult and dispense the rules of government, the plebeians submit to and obey them'.

SIR THOMAS ASTON, 1641

In 1640, England was still a predominantly agricultural society of small peasant farmers. Manufacture was carried on in small workshops, which were generally in the home of the craftsman or artisan, and it was often combined with farming. The country was ruled by a class of great landowners. The revolution was precipitated by divisions within that ruling class, but its character was shaped by the intervention of the 'middle sort of people'. It is necessary to begin by identifying these two social groupings.

The Ruling Class

At the top of English society there was a hierarchy of peers (dukes, marquises, earls, viscounts and barons – members of the House of Lords) and gentry (baronets, knights, esquires and gentlemen). 'Gentleman' had two meanings: it was the title of a man in the lowest rank of the gentry, but it also described the status of all peers and gentry and that which distinguished them from all the rest of the population, the plebeians. While all the peers may be allocated to the ruling class, the gentry were more diverse, differing greatly in wealth and power. Greater gentry, like peers, were big landowners who lived off the rents of tenants, but minor gentry had much smaller estates and were mostly farmers. The ruling class largely consisted of peers and greater gentry, and these will be termed the aristocracy. This is not a rigid or insurmountable distinction: power trickled down from the top to wider layers of society, and many middling and lesser gentry were associated with the ruling class by kinship and by holding offices through which they participated in governing the plebeian masses, as did rich merchants in the towns, but the balance of power lay with the peers and greater gentry. This may be illustrated by more detailed consideration of the most important unit of government – the county.

By no means all the gentry participated in government at the level of the county. In Devon, for example, it was only one-third (Roberts 1985: xviii). Historians differ in their definitions of 'gentry' and 'greater gentry', so their statistics are not strictly comparable, but the trend is clear enough. Out of 679 families of gentry in Yorkshire, the chief county offices – sheriff, deputy lieutenants of the militia, justices of the peace – were filled from amongst the 73 who were greater gentry (Cliffe 1969: 30). Out of 774 families of gentry in Lancashire, 153 were greater gentry and these were 'the real governors' of the county: 'Between 1625 and 1642 all justices of the peace, deputy lieutenants, sheriffs and militia officers were chosen from the greater Lancashire gentry ...' (Blackwood 1978: 10–11).

Other historians identify a small elite group of 'magnates' and a larger group of leading gentry, for example in Somerset:

> At the top of the social hierarchy were about twenty-five families. The head of each was generally, though not invariably, a knight ... It was to this group that the king and council looked for leadership in local government, that the county looked for its representatives at Westminster ... Pre-eminent in land, wealth, and, above all, social standing, they dominated the rural bench and furnished almost all of the deputy lieutenants. These were the county's magnates.

Associated with them were 75 leading gentry families from which came the majority of the justices of the peace, but '... they did not wield the power and influence in the county and at Westminster that the greatest men did, and this was the feature that most clearly distinguished them from the magnates' (Barnes 1961: 11–12). The line is imprecise between greater and middling gentry, but the mass of the gentry were minor gentry whose power and influence did not extend beyond the parish in which they lived (Everitt 1966: 33–5). In Sussex the structure of power is described as follows:

> A few magnate families constituted a ruling elite; many middling gentry owned estates in several parishes and exerted influence beyond their own village; other lesser men were essentially parish gentry, men who dominated their own tiny community but were of little account in the shire. The distinctions within the gentry community therefore are nearly as important as the vital distinction on which everything in seventeenth-century society was based, between the gentry and the people. (Fletcher 1975: 22, 25.)

Thus, while the gentry as a whole were socially superior to the plebeians, they formed a status grouping and not a class, and the majority of them were not part of the ruling elite. That elite,

together with the peers, was rooted in its larger possessions of land
and its greater political power, and so constituted the ruling class.

'The Middle Sort of People'

The largest class in society was composed of small producers. In
agriculture, the predominant element in the economy, these were
peasant farmers and in industry these were craftsmen and artisans.
They were independent small producers in that, and so long as,
they did not work for wages but were self-employed, and in that,
and so long as, they had property and were in possession of the
means of production. In agriculture that meant land and the instruments of husbandry and in industry it meant the tools, raw materials
and finished products of the trade. But from amongst the small
producers two new classes were in process of formation – a bour-
geoisie and a proletariat.

The main changes in society were taking place in its middle ranks.
Some peasants were growing richer by acquiring larger holdings,
employing wage-labour and producing for the market, or combining
farming with manufacture in which they employed their poorer
neighbours. In village after village the middle range of holdings was
disappearing and being replaced by a few large farms and many
small holdings. Often this restructuring of society was brought
about by the development of industry. Some farmers became
wealthy, for example, by engaging in coalmining in County Durham,
or clothmaking in Gloucestershire. In the latter case David Rollison
demonstrates that the bigger farmers of the Vale of Berkeley were
occupied in the cloth industry as well as in agriculture. They
travelled to London to sell their cloth and so widened their horizons
and fell under new intellectual influences, and as they accumulated
more wealth and land they became more independent of their traditional social superiors. (Levine and Wrightson 1991; Rollison 1992:
1–2, 7, 17–18, 43, 86–7.)

John Ashe is an example of a rising capitalist. The son of a
Somerset clothier, in 1625 he settled in the village of Freshford
near Bath, bought land and cottages and established a family firm
manufacturing cloth, employing a large workforce. A regular
income from his land and dairy farming provided capital and
stability for his cloth business. Under the domestic system, which
prevailed in much of industry, the producers worked in their own
homes rather than in factories. Ashe put out work to 'hundreds of
families for carding, dyeing, spinning and weaving before bringing
the cloth back to Freshford for fulling in his own mill ...'. He claimed
that 'the livelihoods and welfare of thousands of poor people, his

workfolks' depended on him. By 1656 he was said to have an income of £3000 a year and assets of £60,000 (Wroughton 1992: 29–35).

A crucial development was the emergence of capitalism from among the small producers. It was a process by which the growth in the resources of a peasant became 'sufficient to cause him to place greater reliance on the results of hired labour than on the work of himself and his family, and in his calculations to relate the gains of his enterprise to his capital rather than to his own exertions ...'. It further involved the rise from amongst the craftsmen of an element which accumulated capital and invested it in employing other craftsmen. (Dobb 1946: 60–2, 125–9, 134–5, 160–1; Hilton 1976: 57–67, 165–9.)

While a few farmers increased their holdings and a few craftsmen expanded their enterprises, the numbers of 'cottagers' – landless or near-landless people – increased. At Terling in Essex, probably more than half of the adult men in the seventeenth century had no other land than the garden plots attached to their cottages, and they worked as wage-labourers for the substantial farmers (Wrightson and Levine 1979: 28, 31–42, 64). In Gillingham Manor, Dorset, in 1624, there were 202 tenants of whom 99 held only cottages with less than one acre. A similar situation existed on the manor of Mere, where over half of the 98 tenants held only cottages with less than an acre. At both Gillingham and Mere the number of cottagers continued to grow and most of them were probably employed in the cloth industry (Sharp 1980: 159–60). At Whickham in County Durham the number of tenants of the manor 'who held only a house or cottage and/or gardens, garths, and tiny parcels of land of less than one acre' increased from 26 in 1600 to 66 in 1647. By the latter year two-thirds of the tenants had little if any land of their own and worked in the coal industry (Levine and Wrightson 1991: 137–41). Deprived of possession of the means of production in the form of land, a class was emerging that depended increasingly on wages for livelihood and fell into the category which contemporaries described as 'the poor'.

Among the peasantry, small farmers were called 'husbandmen' and larger farmers were titled 'yeomen', but the distinction between the yeomen and the minor gentry was blurred. Between the greater gentry and the yeomanry there was a wide gulf, yet between the well-to-do yeomen and their neighbours of the minor gentry there was little difference in income, mode of living and social intercourse. Often a man is described in one document as a yeoman and in another as a gentleman. This reflected the fact that, during the century before the revolution, yeomen rose regularly into the minor gentry, and minor gentry often fell back into the yeomanry. Stephen Roberts finds about 400 undoubted gentry families in Devon and another 150–180 families in a 'transition zone ... in which gentleman could slide imperceptibly into yeoman and back again' (Roberts 1985: xviii). Between 1562 and 1634, 78 additional gentry families were recorded in Lincolnshire, of these 24 came from other counties and amongst the remaining 44 at least 20, possibly 22, came from yeoman stock (Campbell 1960: 38). In Yorkshire, 102 men obtained recognition from the heralds as gentlemen between 1558 and 1642 and roughly half of them were yeoman farmers (Cliffe 1969: 19). In Lancashire 210 families entered the gentry and most of them probably rose 'on the profits of yeoman farming' (Blackwood 1978: 21). Thus many minor gentry were, until recently, yeomen and many yeomen were on their way to becoming minor gentry.

While the line was fluid between the richer farmers and the minor gentry, the better-off villagers were becoming more conscious of the increasing numbers of poor people and of the need to relieve and control them in order to prevent disorder. As payers of the poor rate and administrators of poor relief they tended to differentiate themselves increasingly from 'the poor'. The emergence of 'the poor' as a large and permanent category in perceptions of the social structure led in the later sixteenth century to descriptions of society less in terms of a divide between 'gentlemen' and 'plebeians' and more in terms of a divide between the richer or 'better sort' and the poorer or 'meaner sort', in which the former included the better-off villagers and townspeople as well as the gentry. In the course of the seventeenth century this two-fold classification was giving way to a three-fold classification by the insertion of the category 'middle sort' or 'middling sort' between the gentry and the poor. This reflected the economic and social changes taking place before the revolution, with the growth of substantial farmers as a result of the amalgamation of small farms into larger units and the increase of prosperous tradesmen and manufacturers as a result of commercial and industrial expansion. It also reflected the growing self-consciousness of the 'middle sort' as a distinct interest set apart from the aristocracy on the one side and the poor on the other. It foreshadowed the revolution, during which elements from the 'middle sort' played crucial roles, and during which this terminology came into greater use in order to describe and explain the conflict (Wrightson 1991).

The term 'middle sort', however, is vague. It refers not only to bigger peasants and richer craftsmen but also to the general body of small producers in agriculture and industry who had sufficient resources to live without having to work for wages. It does not mean that a fully conscious capitalist class had already emerged and it is not synonymous with later usage of 'middle class' and 'bour-geoisie'. The rising capitalists among the small producers were at least partially still enfolded within the broad mass of peasants, craftsmen and traders. A bourgeoisie is in process of formation and the appearance of the term 'middle sort' prefigures this, but without divorcing them from the general body of small property-holders who still retained possession of the means of production – peasants, craftsmen and traders. While it indicates a polarisation between the 'middle sort' and, on one hand, the aristocracy and, on the other hand, the poor, this was softened by association of the richer stratum with the minor gentry and by others experiencing poverty at various stages of their lives and at times of economic depression.

Parish Elites

Historians have increasingly emphasised changes taking place in the structure of power in many local communities in the sixteenth and early seventeenth centuries. This process was one in which a few villagers grew richer and most became poorer, and an elite dif- ferentiated itself from the mass. The parish replaced the manor as the primary unit of local government and the richer villagers monopolised the positions of power in the parish, such as church- wardens and overseers of the poor.

Victor Skipp gives a vivid picture of the dominant group in the Warwickshire village of Solihull in the seventeenth century. 'By Stuart times gentlemen and substantial yeomen had come to dominate local society more strongly than ever before: not only economically, but socially and culturally. While farming out the more onerous parochial duties across the full body of the landed peasantry, a relatively small group of leading families tended to keep the key offices in their own hands', such as churchwardens and trustees of the charity estates. 'Undoubtedly the most convenient place to observe the full complexity of the social structure in a pre-industrial English village was in the parish church, when the local community composed itself into its carefully ordered Sunday tableau – overtly at least – for the hearing of divine service.' The top 29 families owned their pews and sat under the central tower and at the east end of the nave, grouped with the lord of the manor and the minister of the parish. Further back, in the central part of the nave and aisles, the lesser yeomen and the husbandmen rented pews. Behind them the smallholders sat on the common benches, in turn separated off from the landless labourers and the 'decayed tradesmen' on the benches beyond the south door designated for the poor, 'well away from all their betters' (Skipp 1978: 80–2). In the early seventeenth century the new pattern of social relations in parishes was demon- strated in many churches when the seating plan was rearranged to exhibit the superiority of the wealthier inhabitants and parish elite (Underdown 1985: 30–3).

The studies by Keith Wrightson and David Levine of the villages of Terling in Essex and Whickham in County Durham show the development and significance of parish elites such as were to be found in many other parts of seventeenth-century England. At Terling the churchwardens and overseers of the poor were drawn overwhelmingly from the yeomen and wealthier tradesmen, while the lesser offices of constable and sidesman were filled most frequently by husbandmen and craftsmen, 'the labouring poor were almost totally excluded'. The village was governed by an oligarchy of 10 to 15 or 20 to 30 men. They had the highest status, the most wealth and the greatest power. 'The overlap of wealth, status, and power, the common participation in parish affairs, and the myriad of other services performed for one another by the more substantial villagers of Terling surely justifies our regarding these men as a distinct group in village society. They formed a local ruling group that possessed a distinct social identity ...'. Their power was based on their control of land, employment, poor relief, and the machinery of social control. They '... had been detached from the world of their poorer neighbours ...'. The existence of economic and social inequality in Terling was not new, but in the early decades of the seventeenth century it is likely 'that the economic differentiation of the parish elite from the labourers and poorer craftsmen was accompanied by a significant differentiation of attitudes and behaviour'. 'No doubt the ruling group was not without its internal distinctions, between the mere yeoman and the great farmer bordering on gentility ... It was nonetheless a group that was relatively open, into which newcomers might be readily incorporated. For them the key was wealth.' (Wrightson and Levine 1979: 17, 19–42, 103–9, 140–1, 156–72, 176–9.)

At Whickham an agricultural community was being transformed into an industrial one by the development of coalmining.

> While the earlier seventeenth century witnessed the gradual decline into relative insignificance of the manorial institutions that had been at the heart of Whickham's sixteenth-century community, the same period also saw the rise of a novel structure of parochial administration which was to define the rights and obligations of the parishioners in a new way and to create new arenas of participation and interaction. By the 1630s the parish of Whickham was governed by a close vestry of twenty-four men. To judge from the surviving lists of its membership, this was composed of the principal gentlemen and coal-owners of the parish, supplemented by leading farmers and tradesmen. (Levine and Wrightson 1991: 344–5.)

Although in many communities distinctions may not have been so stark between villagers, elsewhere the new elite was in part the product of the development of capitalist agriculture in some areas and of capitalist industry in others. With the advance of capitalism, the manorial court declined in importance and the post-Reformation state gave secular functions to the parish, especially in relation to the relief and control of the poor, making it the primary unit of local government.

Ann Hughes stresses the broad level of participation in local affairs by rich farmers, prosperous craftsmen and small merchants, and how this led to awareness of national affairs and to growth of their political consciousness (Hughes 1991: 69–71, 130). William Hunt considers that at the parochial level the large farmers, minor gentry and clergy 'constituted a ruling class of sorts' (Hunt 1983: 21–3). David Rollison speaks of the gentry 'governing at county and national levels' and the 'middle sort of people' managing the parishes, and argues that together they formed 'a kind of ruling-class bloc' (Rollison 1992: 132–3). Cynthia Herrup puts it that 'there was not a single ruling class in England, but ... several distinct ruling classes' (Herrup 1988: 293), but that is a contradiction in terms. Further, there is a crucial difference between the exercise of power at the national level (the state) and at the local level (the parish) and between serving on various bodies locally and taking the decisions nationally. 'Most high political events', in the words of Ann Hughes, were initiated by the aristocracy, 'at court, in parliament, or in meetings of the county gentry'. But the freedom of action of the aristocracy 'was circumscribed by the involvement of a broader political nation which included the groups often described as the "middling sort" – yeomen, small merchants, prosperous husbandmen and craftsmen – as well as humbler men. These members of the broad political nation were well-informed about political and religious issues' (Hughes 1991: 71).

Parish elites represented a potential challenge to the control of the state by the ruling class of peers and greater gentry. They were not a part of the ruling class but the embryo of a new ruling class.

Opposition from 'Middling Sort'

In the 1630s the political consciousness of many of the 'middling sort' was intensified by the policies of Charles I's government. Two examples of this are reactions to the levy of shipmoney and to the conversion of communion tables into altars.

Taxation required the consent of parliament but shipmoney was imposed without that consent, in order to provide ships for the navy, and, although it was not technically a tax, it became in effect annual taxation. The constitutional implications of this worried some of the peers and gentry but it hit the pockets mainly of the 'middle sort'. It extended national taxation for the first time to many of the 'middle sort', and its assessment alienated them not only from the government but also from the rich who it was alleged did not pay their fair share. Opposition to shipmoney appeared first among the middle sort. At Enfield in Middlesex, for instance, a group of yeomen obstructed the levy and they complained that the sheriff shifted the burden from wealthy London merchants and government officials, who had settled recently in the parish, to the farmers. William Prynne, a lawyer who came to symbolise resistance to the regime of Charles I, wrote a tract against shipmoney, in which he said that the main objection to it was the inequality of assessments: '... in the country ... some farmers pay more than the richest knights and gentlemen' and in towns 'the middle and poor sort of people paid more than the richest', 'ordinary merchants' paying more than the richest landowners 'who had forty times greater estates and annual revenues ...'. (Campbell 1960: 368; Fletcher 1975: 205–9; Morrill 1976: 25–8; Pam 1977: 8.)

William Laud, Archbishop of Canterbury, who carried out the king's religious policies, was accused of undermining the protestant religion of the English church by introducing 'popish innovations'. The most visible instances concerned the positioning of the communion table and the procedure for receiving communion. Practices varied locally but it was common for the communion table to stand in the middle of the chancel. The king and Laud ordered it to be removed to the east end and placed behind rails like an altar, and some bishops and clergy required the people to come up to the rails and kneel to receive communion. Thus precedence was given to the altar over the pulpit, and the emphasis of religion was shifted from the sermon to the sacrament. For many Protestants the erection of an altar and the kneeling at the rails implied the 'popish superstition' that the bread and the wine at communion were converted miraculously into the body and blood of Jesus Christ. The minister was distinguished from the congregation by wearing a surplice, to which many Protestants objected as a 'popish' practice, and he was further separated from them by standing behind the rails as intermediary between them and God, thus expressing Laud's policy of elevating the status and authority of the clergy. This was resented by many of the laity, especially the educated 'middle sort' who, by their knowledge of the Bible and the strict conduct of their lives, felt themselves the equals of the clergy, and indeed superior to the many ministers who did not reach the standards they expected of them in their private lives or public performance of their duties, particularly in what they considered to be their most important function, that of preaching. Local communities were annoyed by the interference of the central government and its agents – the bishops – in the way they managed affairs in their own parish church. In many places there was strong resistance, led generally by members of the parish elite, to the conversion of communion tables into altars, and perhaps especially to kneeling at the rails to receive communion. But critics of the performance of the clergy covered a wide social range – yeomen, husbandmen, shopkeepers, artisans, labourers and women – though not many gentry. (Hill 1964; Wrightson and Levine 1979: 161; Green 1979; Sharpe, Jim 1986; Tyacke 1987: 199–209; Sharpe, Kevin 1992: 335–45; Wroughton 1992: 61–2.)

Fear of 'popish' influences in church and state grew. People and nations find their identity in opposition to real or imagined enemies: anti-popery, which did so much to animate the coming revolution, was an expression of Protestant identity and indeed of English identity, shaped in the struggle for survival against the great Catholic powers abroad and their fifth column of mostly concealed 'papists' at home. 'Popery' was associated with arbitrary government and monarchical tyranny on the continent, and with societies composed of a few great lords and a mass of impoverished peasants, lacking the freedom which was deemed the inheritance of Englishmen, and without the strong presence of such as the 'middling sort' who saw themselves as the backbone of England. Groups among English Protestants had long been concerned that the reformation of religion was as yet incomplete, and that the church still needed to be purged of all the 'remnants of popery', such as various ceremonies in the liturgy, bowing at the name of Jesus, and representations of the godhead on crucifixes and in stained-glass windows. But under Charles I and Laud the situation became worse because it seemed that rather than going forward to reformation the country was slipping back into 'popery' and its corollary of royal tyranny.

Recent historians have argued that opposition to the policies of Charles I in the 1630s has been exaggerated, and that opponents of his regime in the 1630s did not necessarily line up against him in the Civil War. The latter is undoubtedly true, the former less proven, and there did exist a continuity of opposition at a popular level in many localities from the 1630s to the Civil War. For example, Barnstaple in Devon was a centre of religious opposition in the 1630s and of resistance to shipmoney, and in the Civil War it became strongly parliamentarian (Stoyle 1994: 174, 179–80, 192–6). At Enfield in Middlesex farmers who resisted shipmoney also opposed levies for the war in which the king tried to enforce his religious policies on the Scots in 1640, and they supported parliament at the outbreak of the Civil War in 1642. William Billings, churchwarden in 1636, refused to bow at the name of Jesus on the grounds that 'may be this was near Rome'. In 1640 he would not pay the levy for raising soldiers to fight the Scots because he was not satisfied it was lawful, and in 1642 he contributed £20 voluntarily to the parliamentarian cause (Pam 1977: 3–9).

CHAPTER 2

The Collapse of the Government

> But actions of that nature, where the people, of their own
> accords, in a seeming tumultuous manner, do express their liking
> or dislike of matters in government ... work ... either to a sense
> causing reformation, or to an hatred of them ...
>
> THOMAS MAY, 1647

In the seventeenth century, England, Scotland and Ireland were
three distinct kingdoms, linked together under the rule of the same
king and thus forming a 'multiple' or 'composite' monarchy similar
to Spain. It is argued that such a structure was the cause of unstable
states in early modern Europe and led to the crisis of the English
state in the middle of the seventeenth century, rather than any
grievances internal to England being of sufficient severity to bring
down the government or to provoke civil war (Russell 1987). The
impact upon England of events in Scotland and Ireland were
important factors, but they increased, rather than caused, the
tensions and conflicts within England. The instability of the 'British'
'multiple monarchy', unlike Spain, was caused by religious differences within and between the three kingdoms, with a Roman
Catholic majority in Ireland and Roman Catholic minorities in
Scotland and England, with a Presbyterian majority in Scotland
and Presbyterian minorities in England and Ireland, and with the
Church of England torn between different interpretations of its
Protestant inheritance. Ireland was less of an autonomous kingdom
than Scotland and more of a dependency, on its way to being a
colony linked to a chain of English imperial expansion across the
Atlantic to the Americas. The 'British' 'multiple monarchy' was
stable so long as its sovereign had a secure and powerful base in
England to manage relations with Scotland and Ireland. The
crumbling of Charles I's power in England opened the way for
Scottish and Irish interventions in English affairs in attempts to
promote their own interests and to secure their autonomy. When
a strong state was re-established in England in the 1650s Ireland
and Scotland were forcibly and ruthlessly subordinated to England.

The collapse of the government of Charles I in 1640 was triggered
by a rebellion in Scotland. Scotland had its own privy council,
parliament, laws and church. It was not integrated into England

as a province, like Wales, and neither was it a dependency of England, approximating to a colony, like Ireland: Scotland was concerned to avoid either of those fates. Charles I's attempts to bring about greater uniformity in religion, both within Scotland and between Scotland and England, by imposing a new service-book on the Scottish church, raised questions both about the survival of the Presbyterian religion in Scotland and about the extent of the power of the crown in Scotland, and led to the revolt of the Scots in 1638. Charles sought to restore his authority in his northern kingdom by force of English arms, fanning fears that Scotland would be reduced to a province of England. In resisting the king's ecclesiastical policies the Scots aroused sympathies in England from the various groups which had been opposing similar policies there during the 1630s. The Scots abolished episcopacy and restricted the powers of the crown, thus providing models for remedying grievances in England.

The king summoned an English parliament to meet in April 1640 in order to raise money to finance the army he was levying to invade Scotland, but it brought forward grievances such as shipmoney and delayed the grant of money, so that after only three weeks the king dissolved it, and it acquired the nickname of the 'Short Parliament'. This stirred and focused opposition in England. Charles continued his effort to raise an army for war against the Scots but was impeded by widespread and serious popular disorders. The levying of conscripts and of money to clothe them might in any case have aroused resistance, but significantly the disorders also expressed opposition to the religious policies of the king and Archbishop Laud in England and sympathy with the resistance in Scotland to similar policies there. The rebellion of the Scots did not create the discontent in England but it gave it the opportunity and incentive to express itself in popular disorders, which undermined the monarchy in England in 1640. The success of the Scottish rebellion was due in the end to the crippling by popular resistance in England of the king's attempt to suppress it.

Popular Resistance, 1640

The immediate popular reaction to the dissolution of the Short Parliament was to blame Archbishop William Laud. On the evening of 11 May 1640 hundreds of apprentices and 'base people' gathered in St George's Fields, Southwark (the large industrial suburb of London) in response to a call to hunt 'William the Fox', who 'seeks to bring this whole land to destruction', by introducing 'popish' practices into the church. They marched on the Archbishop's palace at Lambeth, led by John Archer, a glover, beating a drum.

Laud fled across the river and took refuge in Whitehall and, its prey having escaped it, the mob expressed itself by cursing him and breaking his windows. Archer was arrested, tortured, and executed as a traitor. (Gardiner 1899: vol IX: 132–4, 141; Pearl 1961: 107–8; Tyacke 1987: 237; Sharpe, Kevin, 1992: 906–7.)

The soldiers conscripted for the war against the Scots were drawn from 'the lowest levels of society' but they continued the fight of the communities from which they came, and through which they marched, against the 'popish innovations' brought in by the king and Laud – especially the removal of the communion table to the east end of churches and fencing it off with rails like an altar (Fissel 1994: 260–3, 274–5). In Hertfordshire and Essex they entered churches, destroyed the rails, moved the communion table back to the centre of the chancel, smashed statues and stained-glass windows and caused some of the clergy to flee for their lives. In Hertfordshire small bands of soldiers attacked at least 16 churches. At King's Walden, 24 soldiers entered the church on a Sunday during morning service

> and sat in the chancel till the sermon was ended, and then, before all the congregation, they tore down the rails and defaced the wainscot, invited themselves to the churchwardens to dinner, exacted money from the minister, brought an excommunicated person into the church, and forced the minister to read evening prayer in his presence.

The earl of Salisbury concluded that local people sympathised with such actions, observing that at Hadham only three soldiers were involved in demolishing a new window in the church, and this 'might easily have been prevented and they apprehended, if the town had not connived at it …'. Sympathy may have gone higher than that. The government blamed the local authorities for not preventing or suppressing the riots, singling out a Hertfordshire justice of the peace, Sir John Jennings, for his remissness, and committing him to prison to await trial by the court of star chamber. The Hertfordshire JPs inquired into the riots but the jury certified that it could not discover the names or dwellings of any of the rioters. (CSPD 1640: 580; CSPD 1640–41: 7, 12, 22, 69–70, 140.)

In Essex, rails were pulled down and burnt at Braintree, Chelmsford, Bocking, Great Braxted, Kelvedon, Great Holland, St Osyth and Elmstead; at Radwinter statues were destroyed, and at Panfield the rector was chased out of the parish. The earl of Warwick (lord lieutenant of the county) and the sheriff arrested a number of the rioters and lodged them in the house of correction at Chelmsford and the jail at Colchester. Those indicted for the riot at Great Braxted came from seven different parishes, showing how military service brought together men who otherwise would not have been joined in collective action. They included three husbandmen, a clothier, a woolcomber, a weaver, a carpenter and a blacksmith – 'a pretty fair cross-section of the middle third of the population', comments William Hunt. But in Hertfordshire the JPs thought that the rioters came from the lowest stratum of society and were vagabonds before being conscripted into the army. (CSPD 1640: 516–8, 522, 551, 555; Hunt 1983: 284–7.)

The soldiers gave expression to the popular hostility towards Roman Catholics, which had political implications because it was alleged that the government was under the influence of 'papists' and that the war against the Scots was fomented by them. The soldiers suspected some of their officers of being Roman Catholics and swore 'they will have no papist commanders'. The earl of Warwick found that the soldiers in Essex were 'very jealous' of their officers 'in point of their religion, they having often moved me that their officers might receive the communion with them'. Francis Windebank, son of a government minister, devised a way to overcome the suspicions of his men by playing up to both their Protestant spirit and their fleshly appetites:

> Finding my men to be very ill-affected to this service, and much slighting all their officers because the country had laid an aspersion on all of us that we were Roman Catholics, so that when I first received them divers of them swore desperately they would soon dispatch us if they found we were papists; but finding their humour, on their first day's march, I desired them all to kneel down and sing psalms, and made one of my officers to read prayers, which pleased them not a little, and being very familiar with them at first, giving them drink and stinking tobacco of sixpence a lb., gained their loves … .

But a company of a regiment raised in Berkshire and Oxfordshire disliked their captain for both his religion and his harsh treatment of them. As they marched through Northamptonshire they mutinied and refused to go further, some saying that 'they would not fight against the Gospel'. What they told other companies revealed the mix of suspicions, rumours and prejudices that excited the soldiers, all springing from distrust of their superiors, except that they were still under an old popular illusion that when the people suffered injustice or mistreatment the monarch could not have authorised it and must not know about it or he would stop it. They said that 'they were going to be shipped and sold for slaves, that the officers had false commissions, that the king gave them no authority, that they should be used like dogs, that all was peace in Scotland, and that was only a pretence to carry them some other where', and that all the officers, including even the commander-in-chief of the army, the earl of Northumberland, were 'papists'. At this the whole regiment of approximately one thousand men disbanded itself and, in groups of 20 or 40, set off back to their homes. The privy council sent down the earl of Holland, lord lieutenant of Berkshire, to pursue and capture the deserters. (CSPD 1640: 476–7, 489–94, 506; Fissell 1994: ch. 7.)

The same year, 1640, 600 men raised in the northern division of Devon were placed under the command of Lieutenant-Colonel Gibson. Lieutenant Compton Eure marched one company to Wellington in Somerset. On Sunday 12 July the soldiers noted that the lieutenant did not attend church and began to mutter that he was a 'papist'. That evening they mutinied and killed Eure 'for his religion', parading his body in triumph through the town. Then they set off back to their homes, and meeting another company on the way persuaded them also to desert. Gibson sent for help to the deputy lieutenants of the militia, who secured the arrest of four men suspected of being ringleaders, but another 20 men came to show solidarity with the accused and thrust their way into the presence of the deputy lieutenants, 'all of them boldly confessing the fact, and vowing they were all equally guilty, and told us to our faces (to use their own words), if we would hang one we should hang all'. The deputy lieutenants were taken aback, and learning that a hundred of the mutineers were still in a body only four miles away, they decided to take no further action until things had calmed down. The king issued a proclamation for the apprehension and punishment of the murderers, and under pressure from the privy council the deputy lieutenants succeeded eventually in arresting 140 mutineers, including all but one of the alleged ringleaders. Those who were examined or sought in connection with Eure's death came from South Molton and neighbouring parishes, a region where opposition to the ecclesiastical policies of the king and Laud was strong before 1640 and where resistance to the royalists would be intense in 1642, thus showing the continuity of the mutiny with events before and after 1640. (CSPD 1640: 476–7, 494–5, 496–7, 506, 509, 515, 579, 583, 613; Fissel 1994: ch.7; Stoyle 1994: 39–40, 168–9, 178, 196.)

Soldiers also continued the fight of rural communities, especially their poorer members, against enclosures. The privy council feared that in Staffordshire there might be a repetition of the incident in the previous year when soldiers threw down the enclosures of Uttoxeter Wood in Needwood Forest. Such enclosures followed from the crown having adopted a policy of disafforestation. Royal forests covered very extensive tracts of land in many parts of England. The local people used these open and unenclosed forests as common, providing them with pasture for cattle, pannage for pigs, wood for fuel and timber for building. At disafforestation common usage was ended. The crown received part of the forest and the rest was allocated in compensation to the tenants of the adjacent manors, in proportion to the size of their holdings, who could prove legally that they had rights of common in the forest. The ground was divided between the successful claimants who enclosed their shares into private plots. The more substantial tenant farmers often opposed the project, not because they were against disafforestation in principle, but because they sought to bargain for an increase in the total amount allocated in compensation for loss of common rights. The position was different for poor cottagers with very small holdings or no land at all, who worked as artisans or labourers but depended for part of their livelihood on access to the resources of the forest. They resisted the project outright, often resorting to violence, because they received miniscule plots which did not compensate remotely for their loss of access to the forest as a whole, or they received nothing at all because they could not establish at law their rights to the use they had made of the forest in the past.

Rights of common had been extinguished in Uttoxeter Wood, half of which had been allotted to the crown and the rest to the tenants of the manor in compensation for their loss of rights over the whole. The land had been divided into individual holdings which were enclosed with fences. The deputy lieutenants were directed by the privy council to take precautions to prevent a riot when they assembled the conscripts at Uttoxeter in July. These conscripts were local men who perhaps had enjoyed use of the wood in the past but certainly would have been aware of the issue, and the deputy lieutenants gave instructions to the constables to have in readiness a posse of armed townsmen to prevent trouble. Despite this, the conscripts went to Uttoxeter Wood and the deputy lieutenants were unable to stop them attacking the enclosures. The next day the chief constable arrived with armed men and found the conscripts still pulling down and burning the fences, but he withdrew after concluding that he could not stop them without bloodshed. The deputy lieutenants and the JPs summoned help from all the townships within four or five miles of Uttoxeter and at length were able to restrain the conscripts and put them under a strong guard until they were marched out of the county to join the king's army in Yorkshire. (CSPD 1640: 373–4, 477–8; Sharp 1980: 142–6, 221–2.)

A regiment of 1200 men raised in Somerset, Wiltshire and Bristol, under the command of Sir John Beaumont, became disorderly as it passed through Leicestershire and Derbyshire. It was reported that as they went through the villages the soldiers asked the people if they had any grievances. In Leicestershire they entered the earl of Huntingdon's park near Ashby de la Zouch and killed his deer. In Derbyshire they threw down enclosures made by Sir

John Coke at Melbourne and burnt his mill. Coke suspected that his neighbour Sir John Harpur hired the soldiers to make this attack and that Sir John Beaumont connived at it, but it seems more likely that the soldiers were set on by the people of nearby Ticknall and Calke who were opposed to Coke's enclosures, for when the next band of soldiers came along they invited them to renew the attack. (HMC 1888: 256–8; Fissel, 1994: 272–3.)

When the soldiers who demolished Coke's enclosures were at Derby they broke into the jail and asked the prisoners why they were there. One said desertion from the army, and was then released, another said debt and they freed him too. The breaking open of prisons was part of the pattern of the disorders of summer 1640, as in London during the riots against Archbishop Laud, and at Marlborough and Cirencester. Houses of Correction, where vagrants and the able-bodied unemployed were incarcerated at hard labour, were also attacked, as at Wakefield where the soldiers broke the windows and destroyed the implements of labour.

Numerous other incidents of popular disorder during that summer could be listed, judged by Mark Stoyle as the most serious in Devon since the Western Rising of 1549, and by Kevin Sharpe as the most widespread and violent in the country at large since the Wars of the Roses in the fifteenth century. Deference towards social superiors and compliance with authority were frequently cast aside, and the power of the state, its officers and its ruling class, challenged. 'Attacks on the earl of Huntingdon's park, Sir John Coke's grounds, the enclosures at Uttoxeter in Staffordshire, or the House of Correction [at Wakefield] suggest class revolt against the symbols of privilege and punishment ...', comments Sharpe, and the attacks on churches came into the same category of 'assaults on the instruments of control and constraint' (Sharpe, Kevin 1992: 904–14; Stoyle 1994: 168–9). These popular disorders created a revolutionary situation, causing alarm in the ruling class and a feeling of power among the people.

An Aristocratic *coup d'état*

The king did eventually collect an army, although it took longer than expected and was smaller than intended, because of popular resistance to the war. Whatever doubts members of the ruling class felt about the wisdom of Charles's policy towards Scotland and the likelihood of its success, the great bulk of them loyally cooperated in raising men and money, and in maintaining order. But the policy put them under pressure and worried them because it led to disorders. (Morrill 1974: 27; Russell 1991: 81–3; Sharpe, Kevin, 1992: 801–2; Fissel 1994: 236–7; Stoyle 1994: 164.)

Although the war was unpopular, success would have silenced the critics and sustained the monarchy, but defeat would be fatal, vindicating the critics and disillusioning the loyal.

Instead of the English invading Scotland, the Scots invaded England on 20 August 1640. This came as a shock to peers and gentry who had cooperated in the war effort and had trusted the judgement of the earl of Strafford, the most forceful of the king's ministers, that it would not be difficult to invade Scotland and defeat the rebels in a summer's campaign. William Ashburnham, a courtier and a lieutenant-colonel in the army, wrote from York that the king's forces were marching towards Newcastle, 'to preserve which it seems is now the height of our hopes, so as you see our mighty discourse of an invading war is turned to the sole thought of a defensive, and the general voice in these parts is – pray God we lose this year no more than Northumberland'. Lord Conway, who commanded the cavalry in the army, drew the conclusion that the policy must have been ill-conceived or badly executed 'which designed so powerful an invasion and was then forced to a defensive war, and that upon all possible disadvantage ...'. 'I fear the state has been very ill-advised', wrote John Lanyon, 'for we have neither money nor hearts to maintain a war, and have drawn our enemy into the heart of our country: I fear they will put us to evil conditions ere we get them out'. (CSPD 1640: 609; CSPD 1640–41: 13–14; SPClar, vol. II: 106.)

The commander-in-chief of the king's army, the earl of Northumberland, had, throughout, been pessimistic about raising sufficient money and men to make war that summer: '... it will be dishonourable to the king and infamous for us that have the honour to be his ministers when it shall be known that we shall be obliged to give over the design'; '... for ought I know we are likely to become the most despised nation of Europe ...' (CSPD 1640: 179, 363–4). On plea of illness he gave up the command and was replaced by the earl of Strafford. Charles I decided to go north and place himself at the head of his army. The Scots swept aside Lord Conway's force in a skirmish at Newburn and occupied Newcastle in the autumn of 1640.

Before news reached London of the defeat at Newburn, twelve peers subscribed a petition for calling a parliament. This placed the focus of this crisis on the relations between the monarch and the ruling class. The privy council met on 2 September to advise the king in the light of the defeat at Newburn. The earl of Manchester proposed the summoning of a great council of the peers to advise and assist the king. The earl of Dorset opposed this and urged the calling of a parliament. Manchester replied that he was 'wholly averse from advising a parliament, and wholly for calling the peers, the council of the kingdom, *consiliarii nati*; Edward III called his great council upon a like occasion; they raised great sums of money without a parliament, and assisted the king: the kingdom will follow the peers'. Some councillors thought that such an assembly would do no more than advise the king to summon a parliament. Lord Cottington said that he was against counselling the king to call a parliament and supported the meeting of the peers, and if they declared for a parliament, it would be more acceptable to the king as the advice of the whole nobility than of just the privy council. The earl of Arundel affirmed that a great council of the peers was 'the only way, the best and shortest way', and the privy council concurred (Manning 1973: 43–4).

Ambiguity remained as to whether this was to be an alternative to calling a parliament or a stopgap until a parliament could meet, and whether it was conceived as a means of continuing the war or of making peace. The letter in which the secretary of state, Sir Francis Windebank, communicated the advice of the privy council to the king, is a most revealing document. It recognised the strength of popular resistance to the war, and the real problem was not so much the rebellion of the Scots as the grievances of the English. It made clear the dependence of the monarchy on the aristocracy and the need for Charles to pursue policies acceptable to the aristocracy as a whole.

> The ground and motive [of this advice] has been the uniting of your majesty and your subjects together, the want whereof the lords conceive is the source of all the present troubles; and they are confident, if your majesty and your people had been well together, the rebels [in Scotland] dared not have thus insolently affronted your majesty and the nation; that in probability the lords being made sensible of your majesty's and their own danger, and participants in your counsels, will be won to lay aside all private animosities and discontentments, and unanimously join to save the monarchy, and to repel the common enemy by a present assistance; that the lords, thus gained, will in all likelihood train with them their friends and adherents and many of the people; besides the satisfaction that is conceived the people will receive by this calling of the lords to your counsels; ... that in outward appearance, considering the constitution of the city and the generality of the kingdom, without some such sweetening of the lords and people as this, it is to be doubted, if your majesty should receive a blow ... monies and forces will be raised very coldly and slowly; and without a voluntary assistance of both these, the kingdom must be in danger; for to force supplies of either in this conjuncture is not held practicable ... (SPClar, vol. II: 97–8.)

The implication of this was repudiation of Charles's management of affairs and of those on whom he had relied chiefly for advice, and it pointed to the aristocracy taking control of the government and placing the king under its tutelage. What is marked is the confidence of the aristocrats that they could control the people – 'the kingdom will follow the peers', declared the earl of Manchester; 'the lords … will in all likelihood train with them their friends and adherents and many of the people …', wrote Sir Francis Windebank – and prevent the people getting out of order by removing their grievances.

Charles agreed to call a great council of the peers to meet at York on 24 September. The earl of Bedford and the earl of Hertford, representing the twelve peers who had called for a parliament, met the privy council and urged it to support their petition, which they said would be endorsed by 'many other noblemen and most of the gentry in several parts of the kingdom'. The council informed them of the king's decision to summon a great council of the peers, and the two earls replied that this might do good providing that it was not intended as a substitute for a parliament or to raise money without its consent (SPClar, vol. II: 110–12, 115).

More than ten thousand citizens of London subscribed a petition calling for a parliament, and similar petitions were preparing in the counties. Anxious to stop this campaign of petitioning, and recognising that the great council of the peers would inevitably demand a parliament, the privy council now advised the king to summon a parliament, and so make it an act of his own will and grace rather than a surrender to the pressure of the peers and the petitioners. As soon as the peers assembled at York on 24 September, Charles announced that parliament would meet on 3 November. (CSPD 1640: 624–5; CSPD 1640–41: 40, 56–7, 60, 67–8, 72, 73–4, 77, 79, 84, 90, 94–5.) Conrad Russell has said that the Scots forced the king to summon parliament, and this is superficially the case (Russell 1987: 406), but the military success of the Scots was due to the crippling of the king's war effort by resistance in England, and to the existence in England of opponents to his policies poised to take advantage of his discomfiture at the hands of the Scots.

What was taking place was an aristocratic *coup d'état*. Charles was still under the illusion that he could continue the war against the Scots, but the great council of the peers took control and, led by the earl of Bristol, set up a committee to treat with the Scots for peace. By the time the parliament met on 3 November 1640, since known as the 'Long Parliament', the aristocracy had virtually taken power out of the king's hands: 'In terms of political power, the last two months of 1640 constitute something very like a royal minority …', observes Conrad Russell (Russell 1991: 207–8).

For eleven years, from 1629 to 1640, Charles had not called a parliament, but his government had an aristocratic complexion, if anything, more so than it had previously. The king defended the privileges of aristocrats, increased the proportion of peers on the privy council from two-thirds to three-quarters, and made greater use of them in the administration of the realm (Sharpe, Kevin 1992: 420). However, in upholding the old order, he also sought to bolster the power of the church, and this conflicted with the immediate interests and personal ambitions of the aristocrats. They were antagonised by Laud's policy of raising the status and authority of the clergy. The archbishop encouraged the parson 'to hold up his head in the presence of the county families'. Clergy were placed in secular offices which were considered by the nobility and gentry as their preserves. In larger numbers than before, clergy were made justices of the peace and Laud's success in securing the most important of government offices, that of lord treasurer, for the bishop of London, William Juxon, marked the high point of greater political power for clerics. This offended the aristocracy and Clarendon, later the royalist politician and historian, wrote:

> This unseasonable accumulation of so many honours upon them, to which their function did not entitle them (no bishop having been so much as a privy councillor in very many years), exposed them to the universal envy of the whole nobility, many whereof wished them well as to all their ecclesiastical qualifications, but could not endure to see them possessed of those offices and employments, which they looked upon as naturally belonging to them .... (Hill 1956: 221–3, 340–2; Sharpe, Kevin 1992: 292–3, 399–401.)

The main aim of the aristocrats in the Long Parliament was to rein in the king and make him more dependent on themselves, by removing his chief advisers, such as Laud and Strafford, and replacing them with some of their own number. They initiated a programme of reforms that made them popular, addressing common grievances and not too blatantly pursuing the interests of their own class. When the Long Parliament met it made shipmoney, and various ways of raising money without the consent of parliament, illegal; it abolished the court of star chamber and the court of high commission, which had played large parts in enforcing the king's policies in state and church; and it required that a parliament be called at least once in every three years. The Long Parliament sought to reduce the power of the bishops and to exclude the clergy from secular offices such as government minister, privy councillor and justice of the peace. In order to overcome the king's resistance to the curtailing of his power and that of the bishops, the aristocrats

needed popular support, but that laid them open to popular pressure
to go further and faster than they intended.

The People and the Long Parliament, 1641

One of the first acts of the Long Parliament was to release William
Prynne (a lawyer), Henry Burton (a clergyman) and John Bastwick
(a physician) from the prisons to which they had been sent by the
court of star chamber in 1637 for libelling the bishops. Their pam-
phleteering against the reintroduction of 'popish' practices into the
church, and the pillorying, mutilating and imprisoning of them,
elevated them in the eyes of many to the rank of Protestant martyrs.
Their liberation was the occasion for popular demonstrations
against Laud's regime. On 28 November 1640 Prynne and Burton
were met at Brentford and escorted into London by more than a
hundred coaches and thousands of men and women, on horse and
on foot, carrying branches of rosemary 'for remembrance' and
laurel 'in token of joy and triumph'. In the city, crowds lined the
streets, 'the common people strewing flowers and herbs in the
ways as they passed, making great noise and expressions of joy for
their deliverance and return'. 'It was a kind of triumph, the people
flocking together to behold them, and receiving them with accla-
mations, and almost adoration, as if they had been let down from
heaven.' A few days later Bastwick was met at Blackheath by
another large crowd and escorted into London amidst similar
demonstrations of joy. (Manning 1991:51)

Clarendon thought that the crowds consisted of 'multitudes of
people of several conditions', including 'many citizens of good
estates'. Peter Heylyn attributed the demonstrations to religious
opponents of the government in London and Southwark, and it
was said that the cheers of the crowds were mingled with 'loud and
virulent exclamations against the bishops who had so cruelly
prosecuted such godly men'. It is clear enough that these were
demonstrations by religious enthusiasts in favour of reform of the
church. Nehemiah Wallington, a turner, who lived in Little
Eastcheap in the city, rejoiced at the return of 'those worthy and
dear servants of God'; and Robert Woodford, an attorney from
Northampton, wrote in his diary:

> Oh, blessed be the Lord for this day! This day those living holy
> martyrs Mr Burton and Mr Prynne came to town, and the
> Lord's providence brought me out of the temple to see them.
> My heart rejoices in the Lord for this day; it's even like the return
> of the captivity from Babylon.

Clarendon's description of this peaceful and orderly demonstration
as an 'insurrection (for it was no better) and frenzy of the people'

seems a travesty until seen from the viewpoint of aristocrats horrified at popular intervention in matters belonging to government and parliament. The demonstration was assumed to be against the courts of star chamber and high commission and to put pressure on parliament and the king to abolish them, which indeed it did help to accomplish. It at once raised the dilemma for aristocrats when they summoned up popular support: the expectations of the people were aroused but how far could they be satisfied without endangering aristocratic hegemony, and how far could popular intervention in politics be allowed in 'actions of that nature, where the people, of their own accords, in a seeming tumultuous manner, do express their liking or dislike of matters in government ... ?' (Manning 1991: 51–3).

The aristocracy was happy to throw Archbishop Laud overboard. He was impeached by the House of Commons and dispatched to prison in the Tower of London. As he was being taken there in a coach, Laud related that in Cheapside '... one 'prentice first hallooed out; more and more followed the coach, the number still increasing as they went, till by that time I came to the Exchange, the shouting was exceeding great. And so they followed me with clamour and revilings, even beyond barbarity itself ...'. He was cursed as a traitor and some said they would kill him, so that the Lieutenant of the Tower had to call out the yeomen of the guard to protect him. (Manning 1991: 57; Fletcher 1981: 6.)

The institution of monarchy was protected by the convention that kings were not blamed for the failures or the abuses of their governments, but their ministers were. Besides Laud the other pre-eminent 'evil counsellor' was the earl of Strafford. The only way under the constitution to be rid of him was to convict him of being a traitor. The House of Commons impeached him for treason and that meant a trial with the Commons as prosecutors and the House of Lords as judges. But many of the Lords were not convinced by the evidence of Strafford's treason, and so the Commons passed a bill of attainder which did not require a trial but simply the consent of the Lords and the king to the execution of the earl. In May 1641 thousands blocked Westminster for two days calling for justice and the death of Strafford. It is likely that this helped to persuade the Lords and the king to consent to the bill of attainder. On 12 May Strafford was beheaded in front of a vast crowd, and one who had been opposed to the proceedings against him described the popular rejoicings:

> And to show, how mad this whole people were, especially in and about this then bloody and brutish city (London); in the evening of the day, wherein he was executed, the greatest demonstrations of joy, that possibly could be expressed, ran

through the whole town and counties hereabouts; and many, that came up to town on purpose to see the execution, rode in triumph back, waving their hats, and with all expressions of joy, through every town they went crying, 'His head is off! His head is off!' and in many places committing insolencies upon, and breaking the windows of those persons, who would not solemnise the festival with a bonfire. So ignorant and brutish is a multitude. (Manning 1991: 57–69; Fletcher 1981: 13–15; Russell 1991: 293–7.)

Getting rid of the king's ministers commanded widespread aristocratic support, but the Long Parliament was also confronted by demands for the abolition of bishops, changes in church government and reforms of church services and ceremonies. As John Morrill says, the anti-episcopal campaign 'was essentially a popular movement enjoying the support of a few ministers and gentlemen ...' (Morrill 1974: 20–1). Very few of the aristocrats intended to throw the bishops overboard, and most of them looked no further than reduction in the power of the episcopate and the removal of Laudian 'innovations' from the church.

Early in November 1640 a petition for the abolition of episcopacy, 'root and branch', was drawn up in London and signed by 15,000 citizens. On 11 December it was taken to the House of Commons by 'a world of honest citizens, in their best apparel', numbering 1200–1500. It was delivered without tumult or disorder, so it was claimed, and at a word from the House the petitioners departed quietly to their homes. But one of the king's ministers told the House that he was 'scandalised that such a great number of the city came into Westminster Hall with the same petition'. The issue in parliament became the extent to which popular demonstrations should be allowed and popular demands taken into account. Lord Digby, Member of Parliament for Dorset, thought that 'the manner of the delivery' of the petition was 'a thing of the highest consequence':

I am confident, there is no man of judgement, that will think it fit for a parliament, under a monarchy, to give countenance to irregular, and tumultuous assemblies of people, be it for never so good an end: besides, there is no man of the least insight into nature, or history, but knows the danger, when either true or pretended stimulation, of conscience, has once given a multitude agitation ... .

He condemned the petition for its great presumption in prescribing to a parliament what it should do and how it should do it, and 'for a multitude to teach a parliament' what is and what is not the government of the church according to God's word (Manning 1991: 53–6).

Thomas Warmstry, a clergyman, gave voice in *Pax Vobis or a Charm for Tumultuous Spirits* (1641) to the view of the ruling class about the proper relationship between the people and the parliament. He warned Londoners not to disturb parliament with 'uncivil or distempered concourses, or by any rude or immodest clamours', nor to subject it to 'any unseasonable pressures, or tumultuous solicitations' in the great matters with which it was dealing:

> It is not fit for you to trouble yourselves and them in this kind, because of your different constitution, and various interest you have in the business. That your constitution is different from their's ... it is well if you have enough [wisdom] to steer you right in your private and mechanical affairs, which is your proper station or calling, and you may do well to consider, whether you do well to neglect that business God has set you about, to meddle with that you have no calling unto. But they are stars of a greater magnitude, and therefore may move in a higher sphere, and you may be content to receive their influences. I hope it is not in you all to challenge so much light to yourselves, as to judge of laws being made, much less to determine and set down magisterially to them, what constitutions they are to frame ... Let it be your study to live uprightly and honestly in your trades and callings, and to keep yourselves within your limits, and to the conscionable exercise of your proper employments, and not to intrude into what you understand not: if you will needs to be active in reformation, let it be in the reformation of yourselves.

It was to become increasingly an issue whether 'the people' had any right to 'meddle' in the great affairs of church and state. Parliament was composed mostly of peers and greater gentry, who would hear the grievances of the people but decide on the remedies themselves. That was becoming more difficult to sustain, however, in a society in which substantial 'middle sort of people' managed local communities and felt they had interests in the policies of church and state and how they were governed.

Two issues were developing in parallel: one was the attitude of parliament and the ruling class towards pressure from the London mob, and the other was the attitude of the people to reform of their parish church.

Some of the people began to take the reform of their local church into their own hands rather than waiting for parliament, purging it of 'popish remnants' and completing the Protestant reformation begun under Edward VI and Elizabeth I. Direct action was taken against the form of services contained in the prayer-book. In some churches the congregation sang psalms to drown out the service, and in others they tore up prayer-books. At Halstead, a clothmaking town in Essex, during divine service in the parish church, a group of men and women struck the prayer-book from the hand of the curate, as he was about to baptise a child, and kicked it about the church, shouting that it was a 'popish book'. The constable of the town arrested the ringleaders but they were rescued by 'a multitude of people', and it required the intervention of the lord lieutenant of the county to secure the eight chief offenders. On Sunday 8 May 1641 at St Olave's church at the Old Jewry in London, the lord mayor and some members of parliament being in the congregation, as the bishop went up into the pulpit 'in his lawn sleeves and other vestments suitable to a prelate', a hundred 'rude rascals' began to shout 'A Pope! A Pope! A Pope!'. They were ejected from the church by the lord mayors's officers, but in the street outside they called out that the people in the church were at mass and the lord mayor was a papist, and they smashed the windows of the church (Manning 1991: 85–6). Richard Baxter, a moderate reforming clergyman, complained about 'the headiness and rashness of the younger unexperienced sort of religious people' who jeered and derided the prayer-book: 'I have myself been in London, when they have on the Lord's Day stood at the church doors while the common prayer was reading, saying, "We must stay till he is out of his pottage". And such unchristian scorns and jests did please young inconsiderate wits ...' (Sylvester 1696: 26, 39).

In the early months of the Long Parliament the rails were destroyed and the communion table moved back from the east end to the middle of the chancel in many churches in London and across the country (Fletcher 1981: 109–10). The rails were violently pulled down from about the altar at St Saviour's church in Southwark. Those responsible were brought before the House of Lords and condemned to make public acknowledgement of their fault before the congregation, to pay for the erecting of new rails, and to be imprisoned during the pleasure of the House. They were soon released, however and, on plea of poverty, excused from paying for new rails (Manning 1991: 87). On New Year's Day, 1641, in Essex the altar rails of Latton church were taken down by the bellringers and burnt at the town's whipping post, the punishment of the community being thus inflicted on the offending objects as substitutes for the persons who ordered them to be set up. The rioters included servants and apprentices, and one of them said that he tore down the rails 'because they gave offence to his conscience, and [because] the placing of them was against God's law and the king's, as appears by the twentieth chapter of Exodus and about the twentieth verse'. 'Despite the invocation of scripture and statute, however, there was a carnival quality about the Latton affair. A local carpenter brought a barrel of beer into the church to assist the good work.' Soon afterwards women at Sandon burnt the altar rails 'bravely like devils' on the village green (Hunt 1983: 287–8).

In September 1641 the House of Commons belatedly approved the removal of rails from communion tables and ordered the elimination of all crucifixes and pictures of any member of the Trinity and the Virgin Mary from churches. This led to an outburst of iconoclasm. 'On the beginning of October, 1641, at Leonard's Eastcheap, being our church', wrote Nehemiah Wallington, 'the idol in the wall was cut down, and the superstitious pictures in the glass was broken in pieces, and the superstitious things and prayers for the dead in brass were picked up and broken, and the picture of the Virgin Mary on the branches of candlesticks was broken'. Wallington carefully kept some of the broken glass from his church 'for a remembrance to show to the generation to come what God has done for us, to give us such a reformation that our forefathers never saw the like'. A London churchwarden was reprimanded by the House of Commons for exceeding its orders by taking up brass inscriptions and breaking statues on tombs. At Chelmsford the churchwardens replaced pictures of Christ and the Virgin Mary in the east window with plain glass, but in the evening of 1 November a crowd 'in a riotous manner with long poles and stones beat down and deface the whole window', in which were 'the escutcheons and arms of the ancient nobility and gentry, who had contributed to the building and beautifying' the church. William Hunt thinks that this reveals 'some of the social attitudes that underlay popular iconoclasm', for the window 'was a monument to social subordination ...': it glorified the ruling class, sanctifying and eternalising them and their privileged position, alongside Christ and the Virgin Mary. 'Altar rails and surplices were opposed by a considerable number of men of property, but the chancel window was the collective inheritance of the county's ruling class.' The minister, a moderate reformer, preached the following Sunday against 'popular tumultuous reformation, though to the better', and since lawful authority could not reside in the people, their action 'cast out one devil by another, abolishing superstition by sedition'. His sermon split the congregation. A carbine was fired into his study, and a young clothier led a mob into the church and tried to tear the surplice from his back, reviling him as 'Baal's priest and popish priest for wearing the rags of Rome', but he was rescued by his supporters in the congregation (Manning 1991: 88–90; Hunt 1983: 291–3).

This points to the important fact of division in the church. There was not unanimity about removing the rails from communion tables and in a number of parishes a section of the congregation defended the rails (Manning 1991: 89). When a minister at Leominster in Herefordshire moved the communion table from its altar-like position, he reported that 'the common people exclaim much against me ...' (HMC 1894: 76). Popular support for the destruction of images in some places was matched by popular defence of them in others. Richard Baxter gave this account of his experience as minister of Kidderminster in Worcestershire. When he left the churchwarden to take down the crucifix on the cross in the churchyard:

> ... a crew of the drunken riotous party of the town (poor journeymen and servants) ... run altogether with weapons to defend the crucifix, and the church images ... The report was among them, that I was the actor, and it was me they sought; but I was walking about a mile out of town ... When they missed me and the churchwarden both, they went raving about the streets to seek us ... When they had foamed about half an hour, and met with none of us, and were newly housed, I came in from my walk, and [heard] the people cursing at me in their doors ... . (Sylvester 1696: 40–2.)

Mobs attacked 'papists', but other mobs attacked 'separatists' – Protestants who withdrew partly or wholly from their parish churches and worshipped according to their own forms in private houses, their preacher often a layman. When Praise-God Barebone, a leather-seller in Fleet Street in London, preached in his own house to 100–150 people, 'as many women as men', a hostile crowd gathered outside and smashed his windows. (Manning 1991: 72–3, 79–81; Tolmie 1977: 37–8.)

The liturgy of the prayer-book had thrown down roots and established itself in tradition; people had acquired reverence for its symbols and incantations which marked the passage of themselves, their parents and grandparents through life from birth to marriage to death. There were widespread complaints 'that liturgy had been interrupted, neglected or depraved by those who disliked it'. 'The breakdown of order in the church since November 1640 ... brought a reaction into the open in the localities ... Under the stress of religious controversy the attachment of many to the forms and institutions of the Elizabethan church settlement became evident.' (Fletcher 1981: 283–90; Morrill 1993: ch. 7; Green 1979). While divisions were opening up within local communities, king and parliament were under pressure from London crowds.

The House of Commons sought to remove clergy from secular offices but the extension of this to exclude bishops from the House of Lords was opposed by the majority of peers, who feared to create the precedent of allowing the historic composition of parliament to be altered, for if the spiritual lords could be removed so too could the temporal lords. Also, there was fear that it would be followed by the abolition of bishops altogether. Bishops were the instruments by which the king controlled the church and religion, and Charles was determined to retain them and their existing authority. Proposals for the abolition of episcopacy split both houses of parliament. While aristocrats were happy to see the clergy excluded from secular offices and the powers of bishops curtailed, many feared that the abolition of episcopacy, by destroying hierarchy in the church, would undermine the principle of hierarchy throughout society. A section of the aristocracy, though equally wedded to hierarchy, continued to press for exclusion of bishops from the House of Lords, because their votes, with those of the more conservative peers, gave the king an inbuilt majority against further reforms in church and state, although whether these would include abolition of episcopacy was still uncertain. They were prepared to accept popular support to overcome opposition from the king and other peers, but they did not create the popular pressure.

On 28 November 1641 'the factious citizens begin to come again to the House with their swords by their sides, hundreds in companies: their pretence is only against episcopacy'. There was a hubbub in Westminster Hall and shouts of 'Down with the bishops – Down with Antichrist'. The next day hundreds again gathered about parliament, calling on the members as they passed to suppress bishops: they 'never cease yawling and crying No bishops! No bishops!'. They also cried out against the prayer-book. Sir John Strangways was hemmed in by some two hundred people demanding 'his vote for the putting down of the bishops'. The House of Lords directed the earl of Dorset, who commanded the guard on the parliament, to disperse the crowds. Unable to force the people back, Dorset ordered the guard to fire, at which the demonstrators scattered before any shots were actually discharged. Strangways complained to the House of Commons that if the confluence of the citizens about parliament was not stopped, MPs would be unable to come to the House in safety and give their votes in freedom. Edmund Waller 'much inveighed against the Londoners in coming down after so tumultuous a manner, and crying openly No bishop, No bishop'; and Sir John Colepeper 'said that for his part he conceived the late assembling of the citizens to have been a very great tumult'. Sir John Holland was more sympathetic towards the demonstrators, being assured of their good and peaceful intentions, but he warned that 'it has ever been observed in every well governed state as a thing of dangerous consequence to suffer the people to assemble and arm at their own wills and pleasures …'. (This and the next 3 paragraphs are based on Manning 1991: chs 3 and 4.)

There were large meetings of apprentices and young men in London and Southwark and they subscribed a petition in support of the demand of the House of Commons for the removal of the

bishops from their places in the House of Lords. It was delivered
to parliament on 23 December with 30,000 signatures. Apprentices
were drawn mainly from the middle ranks of the population. Their
intervention in politics and their petitioning of parliament, like that
of women soon afterwards, marked an extension of the revolutionary
situation. Only male heads of households had political rights:
apprentices, servants and women had none. In this patriarchal
society not only wives and children were subject to the authority
of the male head of the family but also the apprentices and servants
who lived and worked in his household. Traditionally the master
represented and spoke for his wife, children, apprentices and
servants, but now apprentices, and soon afterwards women, claimed
their own voices in the affairs of the nation.

On 27 December crowds of apprentices and young men came
to Westminster to know the answer to their petition. They set up
a cry of 'No bishops! No bishops!'. The Archbishop of York was
jostled on his way to the House of Lords and his gown torn. Some
army officers were in Westminster Hall and they called out 'Who
says no bishops?', to which the crowd replied 'We say no bishops',
whereupon the officers drew their swords and began to drive the
people from the hall. John Lilburne, the future leader of the
Levellers, collected a group of citizens, some with swords and
others with cudgels, some sailors with truncheons, and more people
with stones. They counter-attacked the officers and put them to
flight. In the House of Lords the bishops sat anxiously on their bench
listening to the roars of the crowds outside. The marquis of Hertford
told them that they were in great danger and should stay the night
in the House, but the earl of Manchester guarded the Archbishop
of York and some other bishops safely to their lodgings, and 'the
rest, some of them by their long stay; others, by secret and far-fetched
passages escaped home'. As peers and MPs left parliament, the earl
of Huntingdon described the scene that met them:

> Ten thousand 'prentices were betwixt York House and Charing
> Cross with halberds, staves and some swords. They stood so
> thick that we had much ado to pass with our coaches, and
> though it were a dark night their innumerable number of links
> made it as light as day. They cried, 'No bishops' ... and looked
> in our coaches whether any bishops were therein, that we went
> in great danger.

The king issued a proclamation banning all assemblies of people
in London and Westminster, and he instructed the lord mayor to
call out the trained bands to restore order, by shooting to kill if the
crowds refused to disperse. But the trained bands, which consisted
of citizens who were part-time soldiers, were generally sympa-

thetic with the crowds and disobeyed orders to muster: that gave
control of the capital to the crowd.

The next day people gathered at Westminster in even greater
numbers. As bishops were rowed over the Thames towards
parliament crowds ran up and down the banks shouting 'A bishop!
A bishop!', and were so menacing that they turned back. Only one
or two bishops succeeded in taking their places in the House of Lords
that day. The Archbishop of York barricaded himself into
Westminster Abbey with a guard of armed gentlemen who clashed
with a crowd led by Lilburne. The demonstrations against bishops
continued for a third day at Westminster and as the crowds passed
the entrance to the royal palace at Whitehall there were violent clashes
with the gentlemen guarding the gate. The citizens abused the
gentlemen as 'cavaliers' (professional soldiers noted for arrogance
and debauchery) and the gentlemen jeered at the citizens as
'roundheads' (referring to the short hair affected by the more
zealous Protestants, or the round caps worn by apprentices), and
so the names of the parties in the coming Civil War were first coined
in the class conflict of street fighting in the capital.

According to a contemporary observer, William Lilly, in a book
published in 1651, *Monarchy or No Monarchy in England*, the
crowds during this riotous Christmas holiday were composed and
motivated as follows:

> ... most of them men of mean or a middle quality themselves,
> no aldermen, merchants or common-council men, but set on
> by some of better quality; and yet most of them were either such
> as had public spirits, or lived a more religious life than the
> vulgar ... and had suffered under the tyranny of the bishops; in
> the general they were very honest men and well-meaning, some
> particular fools or others perhaps now and then got in amongst
> them, greatly to the disadvantage of the more sober; they were
> modest in their apparel, but not in languages. ... As men in whose
> breasts the spirit of liberty had some place, they were even glad
> to vent out their sighs and sufferings in this rather tumultuous
> than civil manner, being assured, if ever this parliament had been
> dissolved, they must have been wrackt, whipt and stript by the
> snotty clergy and other extravagant courses ... .

'... The present hatred of the citizens were such unto gentlemen
especially courtiers, that few dared come into the city, or if they
did, they were sure to receive affronts and be abused.'

The aristocracy was divided less by differences over the
government of church and state and more by the contrary
judgements generated in the classic dilemma of a ruling class faced
with serious popular disorder. Direct confrontation with the mobs
might worsen and extend the disorder, but failure to confront the

mobs might allow disorder to increase; it might be safer to countenance the popular forces and seek to contain and direct them,
but that might not be possible if their aims diverged too far from
those of the aristocrats or became fundamentally anti-aristocratic.
The balance was tipped for some by fear that the king was planning
a coup to be rid of the parliament and reassert his power. The leaders
of the House of Commons were reluctant to take action against
the citizens demonstrating at Westminster because they saw them
as their only defence against a royal coup. They were right. The
king charged five leaders of the Commons with treason and himself
led armed men to arrest them in the House on 4 January 1642,
but, warned in advance, they had fled to the protection of the citizens.
There were mass demonstrations in the capital and the provinces
in support of the Five Members, and the king, fearful for his own
and his wife's safety, fled from Whitehall to Windsor.

The dominant faction in the House of Commons, supported and
perhaps guided by a minority faction in the House of Lords, was
moved by concern to defend itself now that the king had demon-
strated what they had long suspected – his readiness to use force
against his opponents in parliament. There was no standing or regular
army in England – armies were raised for specific wars, as Charles
had raised an army to fight the Scots in 1640 and disbanded it when
peace was made in 1641. The only permanent military force in
England consisted of a local militia or trained bands – part-time
soldiers, officered by the gentry and supposed to be drawn from
the 'middle sort of people' but in practice often from the 'poorer
sort'. The Commons sought to take from the king the control of
the militia. They expressed fears of 'popish plots', and whether they
themselves truly believed in such plots, many of the populace did.
Such fears seemed to be confirmed by the rising of the Roman
Catholic Irish in the autumn of 1641 against loss of land to plantations of English and Scottish Protestant settlers and the threat
of the subordination of Ireland to an English parliament with an
anti-papist and pro-plantation policy. Reports of the massacre of
thousands of Protestant settlers in Ulster intensified anti-papist
feeling in England and fear of plots by English Roman Catholics,
in conjunction with their co-religionists in Ireland and Scotland,
supported by the Roman Catholic powers on the continent, to rise
and slaughter English Protestants and reconvert England to Rome.
The Irish Rising, however, did not create anti-popery in England,
where it was long well-established, rather it focused it at a higher
level of intensity on internal English politics. The king's opponents
linked the 'Attempt on the Five Members' with 'popish plots' and
the Irish Rising, and concluded on a necessity for parliament to
take control of the militia:

> Whereas there has been of late a most dangerous and desperate
> design upon the House of Commons, which we have just cause
> to believe to be an effect of the bloody counsels of papists and
> other ill-affected persons, who have already raised a rebellion
> in the kingdom of Ireland; and by reason of many discoveries
> we cannot but fear they will proceed not only to stir up the like
> rebellion and insurrections in this kingdom of England, but also
> to back them with forces from abroad. (Gardiner 1906: 245.)

The king was believed to be so surrounded with 'popish' counsels,
even suspected of collusion with the Irish rebels, that he could not
be trusted to defend England against 'popish' plots and invasions,
so that the two Houses of Parliament, of necessity, had to take control
of the militia without his consent for the safety of the people.

Popular demonstrations in London overawed or drove out those
members of the Lords unwilling to go along with the Commons.
Thus purged, the upper House now joined with the lower in the
aim of limiting the power of the king, by making him take advice
from a privy council that would be more independent of the crown
than at present. The privy councillors would still be appointed by
the monarch but subject to approval by the two Houses of
Parliament, and he would be bound by the advice of a majority of
the councillors. The two Houses intended to reduce the power of
bishops and to remove from church services ceremonies that were
'unnecessary and superstitious' and offended the more zealous
Protestants. They would consult an assembly of divines and then
formulate reforms of the government and liturgy of the church which
they would require the king to accept. People might not have been
willing to fight a Civil War for such a programme had it not been
compounded with fear of 'popish plots', of insurrections by Roman
Catholics backed by foreign powers, of massacres of Protestants.
Further, the mobilising of popular support for parliament depended
to a very great extent on groups which expected radical reforms of
religion, and those who threw themselves most enthusiastically into
the parliamentarian cause went beyond the moderate aims of the
two Houses.

The Church of England was the established church, controlled
by the state, and everybody was required to conform to it. It
controlled education and the media of communication; it taught
that the monarchy and the social hierarchy were ordained by God,
and that the people must obey those set in authority over them.
But if religion sustained the existing order, it also contained the
potential to challenge it. In a society in which the Bible provided
most of the idioms and images by which people tried to understand
the world in which they lived and sought to give expression to their
thoughts about it, religion offered the most accessible materials for

constructing an alternative world-view. It is true that the church was the guardian and exponent of the hegemonic culture which nourished the old order, but a hegemonic culture contains the seeds which, fertilised by economic and social change and matured by political activity, have the capacity to challenge the established order.

A growing number of peers and greater gentry feared that the intervention of popular forces menaced the ruling class, and they turned to the king as the symbol and defender of the social order. He insisted on maintaining the episcopal government and the existing liturgy of the church. They were prepared to accept that because they were panicked by the appearance, though on a small scale as yet, of Protestant sects which rejected the established church altogether, and of radical elements hostile to the existing social order. They suspected, generally without justification, that opponents of the king aimed to overthrow the monarchy and the aristocracy. Their fears for the social order would have been less influential had they not been combined with support for the existing church, which could command a measure of popular backing, especially since it had been purged of some of the excesses of Laudianism. They could appeal to those strands of popular opinion disturbed by attacks on what they were used to, unaware or uninformed about alternatives to what existed, and frightened by lurid propaganda that the sects and radicals would abolish the family and private property. As fear of 'papists' recruited the par-liamentarian party, so fear of 'sects' recruited the royalist party.

CHAPTER 3

The Outbreak of the Civil War

The war was begun in our streets before the king and parliament had any armies

RICHARD BAXTER

Divisions amongst the Peers and Gentry

A majority of the House of Lords and a substantial minority of the House of Commons withdrew from Westminster, but those who remained continued to act in the name of 'parliament' and assumed the title of 'parliamentarians'. Faced with the ultimate crisis of civil war the ruling class was shattered into fragments: there were militant parliamentarians and moderate parliamentarians, militant royalists and moderate royalists, and large numbers who tried to avoid commitment to either side. It is misleading to describe the latter simply as 'neutrals', for their stance was often based on positive responses to the issues and on political and religious objectives which they shared to varying degrees with moderate parliamentarians and with moderate royalists. Thus there are good grounds for discerning a broad spectrum of moderates that embraced some parliamentarians, some royalists and most of the uncommitted: their common characteristic was that they did not want to see either side, even their own side if they had one, win an outright military victory in the Civil War, but they sought to have the issues settled by negotiation and compromise. Yet underlying the fragmentation of the ruling class was the fact that each fraction saw its own stand as that which was in the best interest of their class. Moderates perceived the outbreak and continuation of civil war as likely to weaken the ruling class, damage its wealth and endanger its power, and its overriding interest should be peace. Yet in politics the centre is always torn apart in polarising crises and moderates were pulled towards either royalism or parliamentarianism, with many individuals at different stages shifting their position either towards or away from one pole or the other. The royalist standpoint was that the best interest of the ruling class lay in the preservation of monarchy and episcopacy; the parliamentarian standpoint was that the best interest of the ruling class lay in enhanced aristocratic control over crown and church. Parliamentarians feared that to

40

confront popular forces held out more danger to the ruling class than seeking to lead, utilise and contain them; but royalists feared that this strategy would strengthen popular forces which would show themselves inherently hostile to aristocratic rule. In a time of popular upheavals many lords and gentlemen felt safer in arms for whichever wide rather than defenceless against mobs (Holmes 1974: 51–2).

Parliamentarians were a small minority in the ruling class. Of the 23 richest peers, with gross rentals over £6600 a year in 1641, only seven were parliamentarians, and since two of these changed sides, only five were consistent parliamentarians (Aylmer 1986: 207, n.4). J.T. Cliffe calculates that at the outbreak of the Civil War there were 700 gentry with estates of £1000 a year or more: out of these, parliamentarians numbered 197 in 1643, falling to 172 two years later due to defections (Cliffe 1988: 45). All the rest were not royalists because many remained uncommitted to either side, but in the ruling class royalists probably outnumbered parliamentarians by two to one (Morrill 1993: ch. 9; Blackwood 1993; Hughes 1987: 142–3, 161–2).

The earl of Southampton became a royalist because, though 'the crown had committed great excesses in the exercise of its power', he thought 'that the absolute taking away that power that might do hurt, would likewise take away some of that which was necessary for the doing good; and that a monarch cannot be deprived of a fundamental right, without such a lasting wound to monarchy itself, that they who have most shelter from it and stand nearest to it, the nobility, could not continue long in their native strength, if the crown received a maim'. The earl of Newcastle took up arms for the king '… to keep up his majesty's rights and prerogatives, for which he was resolved to venture both his life, posterity, and estate; for certainly, said he, the nobility cannot fall if the king be victorious, nor can they keep up their dignities if the king be overcome'. Lord Savile wrote to Lady Temple to explain that he had joined the king because he feared that parliament would lessen the power of the crown 'so much as to make a way for the people to rule us all' (Manning 1991: 321–2). The earl of Dorset's royalism sprang from fear that monarchy, nobility and gentry would be submerged by popular insurrections and the multitude (Smith, David L. 1992: 119). '… The security of the nobility and gentry depends upon the strength of the crown', declared *The True Informer* from the royalist headquarters at Oxford in 1643, 'otherwise popular government would rush in like a torrent upon them'. Edward Symmons preached to the king's army a famous sermon which was published in 1644 under the title *A Military Sermon*:

> A complete cavalier is a child of honour, a gentleman well born and bred ... he is the only reserve of English gentility and ancient valour, and has rather chosen to bury himself in the tomb of honour, than to see the nobility of his nation vassalaged, the dignity of his country captivated by any base domestic enemy ... .

But the question must follow, as asked at the time by the philosopher Thomas Hobbes, why it was that 'the whole House of Lords should not perceive that the ruin of the king's power, and the weakening of it, was the ruin or weakening of themselves. For they could not think it likely that the people ever meant to take the sovereignty from the king to give it to them ...' (Hobbes 1969: 70).

The answer commonly given by historians is that it was religion which split the aristocracy: royalists were content with the existing church now that it had been shorn of Laudian excrescences, but parliamentarians wanted still further reforms of the church. The peers who opposed the king included a few enthusiasts for godly reformation but most showed no great commitment to ecclesiastical reform. Most parliamentarian gentry can be classified as religious reformers, although often on very slight evidence, but there were still many for whom there is no evidence of godly enthusiasm. It is clear that religion cannot be the total or only explanation of the allegiances of peers and gentry. There was a wide range of religious opinions on each side, and a good many royalists were Roman Catholics who can hardly be said to have fought for a Protestant episcopate and a Protestant prayer-book. Many royalists were moved primarily by loyalty to the crown, while many parliamentarians were concerned mainly to prevent the king making himself an absolute monarch (Russell 1991: 471–3; Blackwood 1993; Aylmer 1986: 31–2). Thus constitutional, as well as religious, issues divided the parties, the balance between the two varying from individual to individual. But the process was one by which constitutional and religious issues became intertwined, with royalists identifying defence of the constitution with the preservation of episcopacy and the prayer-book, and parliamentarians identifying reform of religion with reform of the constitution. John Bond preached a sermon to the House of Commons in 1644 entitled *Salvation is a Mystery*:

> God has now so indissolubly interwoven reforming of religion with the settlement of laws and liberties, that we cannot pick off the latter, and leave the former ... but our Father has so wisely ordered the whole, that if we have no reformation of religion, we shall have no more laws, parliaments, liberties nor privileges.

It might be argued that the royalist section of the peers and greater gentry gave priority to ruling-class interests, hence uniting Roman

Catholic and Protestant elements, while the parliamentarian section gave priority to religion. (Hughes 1989: 243–7; Smith, David L. 1994: 104–6, 155–6.) It was more complex than that, however. It is certainly true that, for the royalist section, preservation of the existing church was now seen to coincide with safeguarding the monarchy and the aristocracy, but for the parliamentarian section there was tension, even incompatibility, between their class position and the ideas of many of the religious reformers in their party, nevertheless their sense of the interests of their class coincided with endorsement of reform of religion as the means to win support and to retain the leadership of their party. This is not to deny that these aristocrats were moved by genuine religious beliefs, but it is to say that those beliefs were part of a matrix formed by their social attitudes and their class position, and that their class interests were sublimated by religion and reincorporated as the urgings of their consciences. A significant factor influencing the form of the Civil War was that economic and social changes had reduced the power of aristocrats to raise armies of tenants and dependents, and so initially the forces of both sides were composed of volunteers, though how much pressure landlords and employers exerted can only be surmised. This meant that ideological issues were important because the aristocrats on each side had to persuade people of the justice of their respective causes. Religion built bridges between the aristocrats and the people, and while royalist lords and gentry could recruit support by defending the status quo in religion, parliamentarian lords and gentry could mobilise support by advocating change in religion.

On the surface the outbreak of the Civil War often appears as a struggle between rival peers for control of the militia, the supplies of arms and ammunition, and the places of military strength in the counties. Lord Fairfax for parliament faced the earl of Cumberland for King Charles in Yorkshire, and Lord Brooke for parliament confronted the earl of Northampton for King Charles in Warwickshire. Sometimes old aristocratic rivalries for the dominant position in a county appear to have been carried over into the Civil War, and the factions continued to pursue goals of local hegemony under cover of being for the king or for the parliament, as in Nottinghamshire where the Greys declared for parliament and their rivals the Hastings for the king, and in Wiltshire where the Herberts became parliamentarians and their rivals the Seymours royalists (Morrill 1976: 43–5; Adamson 1990: 101). Struggles between aristocratic factions for dominance in a locality or in the state were the stuff of traditional aristocratic politics, and some peers may well have been unable to distinguish between the cause for which they fought and the opportunities it offered them for the advancement of their own power locally or nationally. The outbreak

of the Civil War, however, involved more than the clash of aristocratic factions, and it will be argued that it was precipitated often
by popular insurrections. Against that it is held that the outbreak
was brought about by one or other of two small bodies of partisans
arming themselves and taking control of a town or a county by
military force. But the attitude of the populace was a crucial factor
in deciding which side it was that took control locally, not least in
the parliamentarians securing London. At the very least military
domination depended on a degree of popular cooperation: men,
money and supplies could not be raised solely by brute force, and
attempts to do that provoked popular resistance which undermined
or crippled the war effort of either side.

Popular Insurrections

In August 1642 the Civil War began in Essex with a large-scale riot
at Colchester, directed against the royalist Sir John Lucas who lived
near the town. He was 'one of the best gentlemen of that county,
and of the most eminent affection to the king'. He was a rich
landowner and 'there were few peers who had much greater estates,
or lived more noble therewith'. But he was unpopular because of
the vigour with which he had collected shipmoney during his term
as sheriff, because of his enclosures, which had provoked a riot in
1641, and because of his obstruction of the town's water supply.
He intended to go with a dozen horsemen to join the army which
the king was raising, but one of his own servants revealed his plan
to the magistrates of the town. On Sunday 21 August two aldermen
of Colchester – John Langley, a grocer, and Henry Barrington, a
brewer – rode out to the clothmaking towns and villages to the north
and west and urged the people to set guards to intercept Sir John
and his party. On their return they persuaded the mayor, Thomas
Wade, to set a watch on Lucas's house. Just after midnight they
observed some horses emerging from a back gate and fired a shot
to warn the town. Word was brought 'that there were a hundred
men in arms in Sir John's'. Drums were beaten to rouse the townspeople, the trained band assembled, and alderman Dan Cole
ordered the beacon to be fired and horsemen to be sent out 'to call
in the country'. Lucas's house was beset with at least 2000 people,
but the mayor put the number much higher:

> There are gathered together, beside the bands, 5000 men,
> women, and children, which I feared might do some hurt. I
> therefore, being accompanied by some other justices and
> aldermen, made proclamation in several places where the
> tumults were, at one o'clock in the night and several times
> since, charging the people to depart. They however regarded

us no more than they do a child, and then we charged the bands to keep careful watch about the house. This they did until daylight.

At dawn 'the rude sort of people' smashed their way into the house. The first person they came upon was Thomas Newcomen, the unpopular rector of St Runwald's, who had intended to go with Sir John to the king. He had quarrelled with his congregation when he denied communion to those who would not kneel at the altar rails. Now the mob 'tear his clothes off his back, beat him with their cudgels and halberds, and with infinite exclamations, carry him in triumph through the chief streets of the town', debating whether to beat out his brains, or drown him, or stone him to death, until alderman Cole rescued him and locked him in the jail for his safety. Meanwhile the crowd swarmed through Sir John's house and outbuildings, seizing 'much armour and many new pistols and carbines ready charged, new great saddles and other warlike furniture', and a dozen horses. They took hold of Sir John, his mother, sister and servants, but the mayor rescued them and conveyed them to his own house, yet 'nothing would satisfy these tumultuous people' until they were transferred to the jail. By now the mob was swollen by people from the surrounding countryside and the plunder of the house was undertaken in earnest. Money, plate, jewels, brass, pewter, books, writings (probably estate documents and records of the obligations of tenants), linen, woollens and household stuff were all carried away. 'A few hours disrobe the house of that rich furniture that had adorned it many years. The mayor and aldermen standing by all this while, but either not able or not willing to conjure down the devil which themselves had raised.' 'They are come to such a head,' protested the mayor, 'being a mixed company of town and country, that we know not how to quiet them. Believe we could not repress them if we had five trained bands, unless they be killed'. Then a rumour spread that two hundred armed men had broken out of a concealed vault, killed nine people, and intended to attack the town. The shops shut and more townspeople rushed to Lucas's house, where, finding the rumour to be false, '... they now spend their rage upon the house, they batter down the doors and walls, beat down the windows ...'; they destroyed the gardens, pulled down the fences of the park, killed the deer and drove away the cattle. 'And now the mayor's care begins to show itself, he sets a guard upon the house ... yet that guard suffered £100 worth of corn (which at first was neglected as contemptible luggage) to be carried out, and the most of it, to their own houses. Another guard he sets upon the prison lest the prisoners should be assaulted by the people who were so much incensed against them.' 'And to show that their rage will know no bounds ... they break into St. Giles's church, open the vault where his ancestors were buried, and with pistols, swords and halberds, transfix the coffins of the dead.' 'The corpses were dismembered, and the rioters paraded through the town with the hair of the dead in their caps.' William Hunt deems this an act of 'social protest' or 'social resentment': '... a crude affirmation of human equality in the face of death, the Great Leveller, as well as an act of retrospective vengeance'. Perhaps it was a symbolic purging themselves from fear of the family and from the deference they had accorded it so long. (Manning 1991: 252–4; Hunt 1983: 261, 271–2, 276, 290, 301–2; Holmes 1974: 35–6; Fletcher 1981: 377–8.)

The crowds of Colchester and the nearby clothmaking towns and villages extended their attacks to 'scandalous clergy' and 'papist' gentry. They caught Gabriel Honifold, the unpopular Laudian minister of St Mary Magdalen's church in Colchester. Years before a scurrilous doggerel had represented him as preferring wine and wenches to the study of divinity, and later parliament deprived him of his living for 'seldom preaching, swearing, and playing at cards and tables on the Lord's Day'. Now 'a multitude of boys and rude people' threw stones and dirt at him until he was taken to the jail for his safety, while the crowd rifled his house of all its furniture and took away 'his bonds, bills, and evidences'. They spread across the countryside attacking the houses of several other clergy, taking away their money, goods, clothes, books and cattle. One party went to the house at Berechurch of Sir Thomas Audley, a Roman Catholic, which they 'plundered of its furniture, and his grounds and pastures of his cattle'. A large crowd went to the house of Countess Rivers at St Osyth, who was a big landowner, a Roman Catholic, and a courtier in the queen's household. She had warning of their coming and fled to her house at Long Melford in Suffolk. 'They enter the house, and ... they pull down, cut in pieces, and carry away her costly hangings, beds, couches, chairs, and the whole furniture of her house, rob her of her plate and monies; they tear down her wainscot, lead, and windows, and they leave not a door, nor so much as a bar of a window behind them.' They destroyed her gardens and crops, spoiled her park, and drove off her cattle. Depositions taken after this affair indicate that most of the rioters were weavers. Such acts gave to the powerless a feeling of power over those to whom they were normally subordinate; they also provided an unexpected holiday and diversions from hard labour and cruel poverty.

The House of Commons sent down the two Members of Parliament for Colchester, Sir Thomas Barrington and Harbottle Grimston, both parliamentarians, to restore order. They reached the town on 25 August and found crowds still incensed against 'papists' and 'cavaliers'. Barrington addressed them in the market-place 'and very lovingly besought the people to do no more', and leaders of the crowd replied: 'If the parliament were safe it was as much as they desired'. The MPs took charge of Sir John Lucas and Thomas Newcomen and said that they would take them to London to be punished as delinquents. A large crowd gathered at the jail when the prisoners were brought out. Grimston placed guards on either side as he hustled them hastily into Barrington's coach, and the crowd showed particular hostility towards Newcomen, but 'the people then not daring to strike or stone him, lest the mischief intended him should light on Sir Thomas Barrington'. The coach was guarded out of town but met with 'bitter curses and revilings' all the way to London, especially at Chelmsford and Romford. (Manning 1991: 254–5; Hunt 1983: 261, 302–3; Fletcher 1981: 378.)

The disturbances at Colchester precipitated 'the worst riots of the century' all along the Stour valley. Sir Robert Crane, MP for Sudbury, reported that the tumults had spread to Suffolk: 'The people in these parts begin to take example by the insurrection at Colchester.' The heart of the disorders lay in the clothmaking towns and villages on the Essex–Suffolk border, and Countess Rivers found that she had jumped out of the frying pan into the fire when her house at Long Melford, near Sudbury, became the main target on 24 or 25 August. She sent her steward to get help from the earl of Warwick – a Catholic royalist looking for protection from a Protestant parliamentarian was an appeal to class solidarity. The earl was at sea securing the fleet for parliament and so his steward, Arthur Wilson, took some men and set out in his master's coach to rescue the countess. He gave a vivid account of his journey through the tumults of the Stour valley:

> With difficulty I passed through the little villages of Essex, where their black bills and coarse examinations put us to divers demurs. And, but that they had some knowledge both of me and the coach, I had not passed with safety ... When I came to Sudbury in Suffolk, within three miles of Long Melford, not a man appeared till we were within the chain. And then they began to run to their weapons, and, before we could get to the market-place, the streets swarmed with people. I came out of the coach, as soon as they took the horses by the heads, and desired, that I might speak with the mayor, or some of the magistrates, to know the cause of this tumult, for we had offended nobody. The Mouth cried out, this coach belongs to the Lady Rivers, and they are going to her ... And some, who pretended to be more wise and knowing than the rest, said that I was the Lord Rivers, and they swarmed about me, and were so kind as to lay hold on me. But I calmly entreated those many hundreds which

encircled me to hear me speak, which before they had not patience to do, the confusion and noise was so great. I told them I was steward to the earl of Warwick, a lover of his country, and now in the parliament's employment; that I was going to Bury about business of his; and that I had letters in my pockets (if they would let any of the magistrates see them) which would make me appear to be a friend and an honest man. This said, the Mouth cried out, Letters! Letters! The tops of the trees, and all the windows, were thronged with people, who cried the same. At last the mayor came crowding in with his officers, and I showed him my letters ... The mayor's wisdom said he knew not my lord's hand; it might be, and it might not. And away he went, not knowing what to do with me, nor I to say to them.

But the town clerk, whose father was a servant to the earl of Warwick,

told the mayor and the people, I was the earl of Warwick's steward, and his assurance got some credit with them. And so the great cloud vanished. But I could go no further to succour the Lady Rivers, for I heard, from all hands, there was so great a confusion at Melford, that no man appeared like a gentleman, but was made a prey to that ravenous crew.

So he left the coach at Sudbury 'and went a byway to Sir Robert Crane's, a little nearer Melford, to listen after the countess' (Peck 1732–35: vol. II, bk xii, 23–5).

By this time the sack of Melford Hall was complete. The windows were broken, iron pulled out, ceilings torn down, 'all likely places digged where money might be hidden', 'beer and wine consumed, and let out (to knee deep in the cellar)', all goods in the house carried off in carts: 'in a few hours' the house was disfurnished 'of all the goods which had been many years with great curiosity providing'. The gardens were destroyed, the corn dug up, the cattle driven away, and the deer killed. The countess herself barely escaped with her life, 'after great insolence had been used to her person'. With the help of Sir Robert Crane, she made her way to Bury St Edmunds, which shut its gates against her at first and then only permitted her to remain there one night. The next day, 'keeping herself as private as she could', she made her escape to London. She put her losses at Long Melford and St Osyth at £50,000. Crane, an uncertain parliamentarian, was threatened by the mob for assisting the countess's escape and 'was forced to retain a trained band in his house ... to secure himself from the fury of that rabble'.

Gifford Hall at Stoke-by-Nayland in Suffolk, the house of the Roman Catholic Sir Francis Mannock, was pillaged of all goods; and, as is said, not his writings spared, which he craved, but were torn, nor his dogs. Also one Mr Martin's house pillaged. Doctor Warren's house was rifled for his gods, and a great many set about the market cross, termed his young ministers. Him they huffed and shuffed about, but (as is said) hurt not otherwise, though he say they took money from him.

(Hunt suggests that Doctor Warren's 'gods' may have been classical statuary mistaken for 'popish images'.) The mobs did not confine themselves to attacking the houses of Roman Catholics, but 'they do plunder divers gentlemen's houses, as well Protestants as papists, and have made great spoil', 'alleging them to be persons disaffected to the parliament'. (Manning 1991: 256–8, 330; Hunt 1983: 303–9; Holmes 1974: 43–5; Fletcher 1981: 377–8.)

On the basis of the fragmentary evidence available, Hunt concludes that 'weavers and rural artisans seem to have predominated' amongst the rioters, 'with a sprinkling of husbandmen and yeomen', but few labourers: women as well as men took part. Arthur Wilson, however, made the significant observation that 'this fury was not only in the rabble, but many of the better sort behaved themselves as if there had been a dissolution of all government ...'.

In the background to these riots was a severe slump in the cloth-making industry. This was a result of the general economic depression occasioned by political uncertainties caused by the deadlock between the king and the two houses of parliament and the prospect of civil war. It was believed by many that Charles had been incited to his breach with the two houses by the influence of the Roman Catholics and so the depression was blamed on the 'papists', who 'were the causes of the present troubles and distractions in the kingdom, and were the occasions that they, their wives and children were brought into great want and extremity, by the great decay of trading' (Holmes 1974: 44–5; Hunt 1983: 293–4). Arthur Wilson, however, thought that anti-popery was a pretence and that 'spoil and plunder was their aim', and his view is not to be discounted entirely. But the breakdown between the king and the two houses of parliament and fear that the rising of Roman Catholics in Ireland would be repeated in England, did cause great anxieties and did lead communities to be frightened of being attacked by 'papists' and 'malignants'. Nevertheless, these were not just food riots and were more than anti-popery riots, for they were politi-cised by the crisis between the king and parliament and motivated by support for parliament. The targets of the crowds were suspected opponents of parliament, whether 'papist' gentry or Laudian clergy, and they claimed to have authority from parliament to search the houses of 'malignants' (supporters of the king) for arms. They deferred to the authority of parliamentarian gentry like Sir Thomas Barrington and Harbottle Grimston. Association with the parliamentarian earl of Warwick carried Arthur Wilson safely through the turbulent villages of Essex and got him out of his difficulties at Sudbury. Barrington reported that the people in Essex expressed zeal for the service of parliament and Grimston returned with 150 volunteers to serve in parliament's army and £6000 in voluntary contributions to parliament's cause. Large numbers of Essex men joined the regiments raised by the earl of Essex and Lord Saye for parliament (Manning 1991: 258–9; Holmes 1974: 36). But it was not quite as simple as that: it is true that the crowds were selective in their targets, however they did not confine themselves to searching for arms, and the violence of their assaults on the property of wealthy landlords is indicative of underlying class hatred, which cloaked itself in legitimacy by choosing for attack those aristocrats who could be identified by reference to parliament's generalised denunciations of 'papists' and 'malignants'. It left parliamentarian aristocrats feeling deeply uneasy.

In the midlands of England during July and August 1642 the royalist earl of Northampton and the parliamentarian Lord Brooke confronted each other, but behind their cautious manoeuvrings and reluctance to fight a different sort of confrontation was taking place. The obituary of Sir John Smith, who rose to high command in the king's army, was published at Oxford in 1644 under the title *Britannicae Virtutis Imago: Or, The Effigies of True Fortitude*. It includes an account of the reality of the outbreak of the Civil War at the level of a village. Smith was a younger son of a wealthy Roman Catholic family in Warwickshire and a professional soldier. His civil war career began with his appointment as captain of the troop of horse raised by Lord John Stuart, brother of the duke of Richmond. At the beginning of August 1642 he was sent with the troop to support the earl of Northampton in Warwickshire. Quartering at Rugby, he heard that the people of Kilsby, a few miles away, midway between Coventry and Northampton, had taken up arms against the king. Before dawn on a wet morning he rode with 30 men towards Kilsby.

As soon as it was clear day he entered the town, where presently he found the people gathering together, some with muskets or other guns, others with pitchforks and clubs. He asked them what they meant, and told them he had no purpose to do them harm, entreating them to deliver up their arms for his majesty's service. The unruly people no whit hearkened to his courteous desires, but furiously assaulted his troop, (which could not be drawn up into a body in regard of the straitness of the passage) they wounded two or three of his men and some horses. Yet made he shift to disarm some of them, and then advances to the constable's house, where he finds more company; but commanded his men not to discharge a pistol upon pain of death, hoping yet by fair means to qualify them. Immediately divers shot is made from the windows at him; whereupon, he commanded his men to give fire, and so presently dispatched three or four of them; which the rest seeing, ran all away except an old man that with his pitchfork ran at Captain Smith, and twice struck the tines thereof against his breast, who by reason of his [armour] under a loose coat received no hurt, yet could not this old man by any entreaty be persuaded to forbear, till a pistol quieted him.

The name of the old man was Henry Barefoot. There might be a question where 'true fortitude' lay in this the first 'battle' of the English Civil War.

The Civil War began with the struggle between the two parties for control of the militias of the counties: each appointed an aristocrat, presumed to be sympathetic, to take command of the militia of a county, under the authority of the militia ordinance in the case of the two houses of parliament and of commissions of array in the case of the king. The earl of Bath received a commission of array for Devon, but the grand jury at the assizes condemned it as an 'extreme grievance and terror to us all', threatening to embroil the county in civil strife. The earl declared that in undertaking the commission he was doing 'nothing contrary to the laws of this kingdom, nor prejudicial, or hurtful, to any that shall observe it'. It was rumoured that by the commission the earl would lay taxes and impositions on the people, but he denied this and said that it was only for their protection. The supporters of parliament replied that it was illegal and was intended to start a civil war in England so 'that the rebellion may prevail in Ireland'. But some of the larger landowners of north Devon urged the earl to execute the commission, and they became active 'to stir up royalist sentiment amongst their tenants and to convince the inhabitants of their areas of the legality and justice of the royal cause'. But many people looked upon the commissioners of array 'as the first instigators of a breach of the peace'.

Setting about the execution of the commission, the earl sent one of his servants to the mayor of South Molton, a centre of the cloth-making industry, 'to know whether he should have a peaceable entrance' into the town. The mayor replied 'that if his intent were for peace, he should come'. The earl entered with Viscount Chichester, Sir Hugh Pollard, Sir Popham Southcott, Sir Ralph Sydenham and several other gentry 'with their followers', and went to an inn for a dinner of venison prepared by the earl's own cook.

The common sort of the town fell in a great rage with the mayor and his company, for giving licence that they should enter, and swore that if they did attempt anything there, or read their commission of array, they would beat them all down and kill them, if they were all hanged for it; and thereupon betook themselves to arms, both men, women, and children, about the cross in the market-place. I do verily believe they were in number at least 1000, some with muskets loaded, some with halberds and black bills, some with clubs, some with pikes, some with dung evells, some with great poles; one I saw had heat the caulk of a scythe, and beat him out right, and set him in a long staff; the women had filled the steps of the cross with great stones and got up and sat on them, swearing if they did come there they would brain them. One thing which is worth the noting, a woman which is a butcher's wife, came running with her lap full of ramshorns for to throw at them … Amongst this crew were both men and women with clubs and staffs, which do daily beg from door to door.

When some of the earl's party approached the cross the crowd set up a great shout 'They be come!'. The royalist gentry and their servants took cover and the earl fled from the town under a hail of stones (Andriette 1971: 56–64).

Lord Chandos attempted to execute the king's commission of array in Gloucestershire. He called the gentry of the county to a meeting at Cirencester, but the townspeople, suspecting that the intention was to proclaim the commission, put posts and chains across the streets to impede horsemen, and sent to the clothmaking districts for help, from which came a thousand armed men. When Lord Chandos appeared on Rendcomb Down he was accompanied by no more than 30 men, armed only with swords, and the parliamentarian gentry went out to meet them and agreed that they could enter the town, provided that they did not execute the commission of array. Chandos and his party went to dinner with the gentry and the magistrates of the town. A large crowd gathered outside and demanded to know why Chandos had come. He came out and told them 'that it was to confer with the gentlemen for the peace of the county'. The crowd called for him to give up his commission of array or they would take him to parliament. The chief townsmen and the parliamentarian gentry, seeking to pacify the crowd, persuaded Chandos to promise in writing that he would not execute the commission, but this did not satisfy the people, who continued to call for him to be made a prisoner and sent to London. There seemed to be a real danger that he 'might have been torn in pieces by some of the enraged country people', and some of the chief townsmen and parliamentarian gentry smuggled him out of the town by a back way, leaving his coach behind in order to divert attention from his escape. When the country people realised that he had eluded them, they 'were extremely enraged, and had like to have pulled down the house' where he had been, but seeing his coach they 'cut it and tore it all in pieces', 'delighting in a contumelious revenge and rustic triumph'. A parliamentarian clergyman in Gloucester suspected that the 'fury that took hold of the ignoble multitude' at Cirencester sprang from the opportunity 'to vent their humours' in reaction to their 'usual restraint and subjection'. Although he was glad that the commission of array was stifled at its birth in the county, he warned that 'prudent men' should 'promote and maintain' such popular uprisings 'yet no further than themselves can overrule and moderate' them (Manning 1991: 250–1; Rollison 1992: 155–8).

The marquis of Hertford was sent by the king to secure the west of England. He made his headquarters at Wells in Somerset and gathered three troops of horse and a few hundred infantry from the militia, making a total strength of nine hundred, but many of the militiamen soon deserted. The parliamentarian gentry raised armed men from amongst their tenants and neighbours, and the Bath regiment of the militia came to them with the addition of many volunteers. The royalist gentry were less successful in recruiting their tenants and neighbours. The parliamentarians claimed that 'there came to us every one' of the tenants of the royalist Thomas Smith of Long Ashton. Although Sir Ralph Hopton had been 'a gentleman very well beloved in the whole county', now that he took arms for the king his popularity evaporated and 'all the inhabitants of that quarter where [he] lives to his very gates' joined the parliamentarian forces, and 'from Evercreech his own tenants and servants come against him and cry him down now ...'. Between 1 and 5 August huge numbers of country people and clothworkers, men and women, from northeast Somerset massed on the Mendip hills, 'some bringing pitchforks, dungpicks, and such like weapons, not knowing (poor souls) whom to fight against, but afraid they were of the papists'. In the end 12,000 people may have assembled. Hertford believed 'that great multitudes of people were poisoned and enraged' against the commission of array by 'false and scandalous suggestions' that its intention was to 'enthral the people' by setting up an arbitrary power and laying immense taxes on them. On the other side it was said that 'the people have resolved rather to lose their lives than to be slaves', believing that if the royalists should triumph 'all should be, upon the matter, no better than slaves to the lords, and that there was no way to free and preserve themselves from this insupportable tyranny than by adhering to the parliament, and submitting to the ordinance for the militia, which was purposely prepared to enable them to resist these horrid invasions of their liberties'. Faced with this great popular uprising the marquis and the royalist gentry fled from Wells to Sherborne Castle in Dorset, the seat of the earl of Bristol.

As well as fears of attacks from 'papists' and rumours about the intentions of the commissioners of array, it is part of the explanation of this popular uprising that Hertford and his party came from outside and appeared as intruders into Somerset, 'incendaries ... and desperate cavaliers' entering armed and threatening the peace and order of the county. But the uprising took place in a region dominated by cloth manufacture and marked by resistance to Laudianism. In the 1630s, for example, the people of Beckington, a clothmaking village near Frome in northeast Somerset, had refused to obey the order of the bishop of Bath and Wells to move their communion table to the east end of the church. When the churchwardens were excommunicated and imprisoned for disobeying the bishop, a thousand local people signed a petition in their support and raised a large sum to enable them to appeal to the Court of Arches. The crowds in 1642 were moved by godly zeal. During the nights they spent in the hills they prayed and sang psalms, and after the flight of the royalists, despite appeals to them not to go to Wells, they 'entered the city with such great expression of joy as is hardly imaginable, gloried in having vanquished the papists, tore down the painted glass in the cathedral, and visited and sacked the bishop's palace'. Organs and pictures were destroyed and a portrait of the Virgin Mary 'was put on a spear and carried about in contempt and derision'. It was more than a movement to preserve the peace of the county and to defend it against an external threat, it was a movement in support of parliament. As John Wroughton says, they wanted peace but not at any price: 'If war were to come, then they knew clearly which side they were on, which leaders they would follow and which principles they would defend.' Traditional deference to social superiors did not explain popular behaviour, because it was withheld from royalist aristocrats, and the gentry they followed were those whose actions they approved. The people of northeast Somerset were predominantly parliamentarian in their sympathies, and although this was submerged when royalist forces from outside conquered the county in 1643, it resurfaced in 1645 in a popular uprising which mirrored that of 1642 and assisted in the final defeat of the royalist party in the west of England. (Manning 1991: 243, 245–6, 263–4, 267–8; Underdown 1973: 31–40; Wroughton 1992: 62, 66, 69–90, 126–32; Fletcher 1981: 363–4.)

The popular insurrections described in this chapter were compounded from diverse elements – economic distress in clothmaking districts and fear of attacks from 'papists', anxiety to prevent the outbreak of war, and concern to protect the locality against incursions from outside or risings from within by armed men bent on war. But historians have gone too far in attributing to these crowds an apolitical localist spirit and indifference or neutrality towards the issues between royalists and parliamentarians. A theme of hostility towards royalists and sympathy with parliamentarians runs through these movements and links them together despite their localised diversity.

In discounting the importance of popular opinions and actions historians have overlooked the nature of the phenomenon they are studying, which is that civil wars spring from deep divisions in a society. Recognition of this allows the traditional picture of the English Civil War to be enlarged, so that it does not arise only from within the ruling class but also wells up from below. While so far attention has been focused on those areas in which the tide of popular feeling flowed against the royalists, there were other areas in which it flowed against the parliamentarians.

When the commission of array was set on foot in Worcestershire, Richard Baxter, the moderate reforming minister of Kidderminster, described how 'a violent country gentleman' called after him 'there goes a traitor', and 'the rabble presently cried, "Down with the roundheads", and some they knocked down in the open streets' (Sylvester 1696: 40–1). Lady Harley, a parliamentarian, chronicled in her letters the widespread popular hostility in Herefordshire towards clergy and gentry who were thought to be enemies of the king (HMC 1894: 88, 89, 90, 92–3, 95–6, 103, 104). At York in February 1642 'two hundred blue ribands' attacked the breakers of church windows, and in March the apprentices and 'the inferior rabble' abused petitioners who came from Lincolnshire to express to the king their fears of 'the designs of the popish party' and to urge him to return to Westminster and 'listen to the faithful counsels' of his parliament. In September 'a great company of the citizens, apprentices and others' marched through York throwing their hats into the air and crying 'For the king! For the king!', smashed the windows of a watchmaker alleged to be a 'roundhead', and threatened anyone who spoke well of the parliament (Johnson 1848: vol. II: 375, 393).

Popular movements involving broad social strata provided the momentum on both sides for Civil War. It is important to stress that neither party in the Civil War was uniform throughout the land but variously shaped by different local contexts. Class antagonism between 'the people' and the aristocracy surfaced in certain areas, especially clothmaking regions, but by no means everywhere. The extent to which the Civil War became a class conflict rests upon analysis of the role of 'middle sort of people' to which the next chapter will turn.

CHAPTER 4

'Middle Sort of People' and Revolution

Why does God prefer his people above all the world? It is not for their birth, their parts, their breeding, but because Christ is formed in them, therefore ... God counts nothing too dear for them ... For your sakes "I sent to Babylon and brought down their nobles" ...

JEREMIAH WHITTAKER, 1643

Peasants and Landlords

Most of the population of seventeenth-century England was engaged in agriculture, as tenant-farmers or farm labourers; and most of them continued at their livelihoods as best they could and tried to avoid being drawn or forced into the war between king and parliament. However, historians tend to underestimate or underplay the extent to which tenants did defy their landlords or were influenced by grievances against their landlords.

On 17 September 1642 the royalist squire William Davenport of Bramhall in Cheshire was at dinner when a letter was brought to him from 24 of his tenants:

Much honoured sir, we your worship's tenants here present, having these many days with sad spirits weighed not only the woeful distractions of our kingdom, but also the present standing that is betwixt your worship and ourselves, have thought it our duty ... to present your worship with these few lines of our humble request: wherein we do most humbly entreat your worship, that either you would be pleased to bend your intentions that way which we may with upright hearts and safe consciences cleave to you both in life and death, which in so doing we shall be willing to do; or else that your worship will not repute us ill-affected or false-hearted tenants in refusing to venture our lives in causes that our hearts and consciences do persuade us are not good or lawful, nor such as we dare safely and with good consciences maintain and defend you in. For, howsoever we would not for the world harbour a disloyal thought against his majesty, yet we dare not lift up our hands against that honourable assembly of

56

parliament, whom we are confidently assured do labour both for the happiness of his majesty and all his kingdom.

Davenport recorded that 'the very next day (and it being the sabbath day too), not staying or belike caring much for me or my answer, they with some others of my tenants enrolled their names and listed themselves with Captain Hyde of Norbury to become soldiers for the parliament under his command' (Manning 1991: 268–9).

Sir George Middleton of Leighton Hall in Lancashire, a prominent royalist, was in dispute with his tenants on the eve of the Civil War over the level of payments (termed 'fines') due on the succession of a new lord of the manor and whenever a new tenant took over a holding, whether by inheritance or purchase. Sir George's tenants regarded the fines he imposed on them excessive and refused to pay. In 1643 or 1644 some of the tenants enlisted as parliamentarian soldiers and Sir George accused them of doing so in order 'to oppose him and his family under pretence of serving the parliament'. Leighton Hall was broken into and plundered by parliamentarian soldiers, who seized documents and gave them to the tenants, advising them 'to take such writings as concerned them if there were any such and to burn the rest ...'. Sir George subsequently complained that the loss of his estate papers made it difficult for him to combat the claims of his tenants over their customary rights. Deeds of sale were destroyed and tenants repossessed themselves of tenements which they had been forced to sell to Sir George (O'Riordan 1993).

The king himself was a great landlord. As lord of the manor of Epworth in the Isle of Axholme, Lincolnshire, he was involved in disputes with the tenants from 1626 onwards over the schemes he promoted for the draining of the fens, which provided common land on which they had rights to pasture sheep and cattle. They were deprived of a large part of their common, which was allotted for the reward of the entrepreneurs who undertook the work of drainage. The tenants were prevented from legal trial of their rights and coerced into submission by the full power of the state. But when the Civil War broke out they formed two companies of foot for parliament, and with arms in their hands took back their common by force. Their leaders were convinced parliamentarians but the main objective of the rank-and-file was probably the regaining of their lost pastures, and as it became clear that parliament did not support them in this they became disillusioned with its cause (Lindley 1982: 23–32, 71–9, 140–2, 146–57).

Large numbers of husbandmen and labourers, however, did serve in the king's forces. It is impossible to say how far they were influenced or coerced by royalist landlords and employers, or how far they made up their own minds on the justice of the king's cause. Although there is more evidence of tenants defying royalist landlords, there are instances of tenants of parliamentarian landlords opting to support the king, which further attests to the fact that numbers of peasants did form their own views about the conflict and did act independently of their lords (Stoyle 1994: 140–7). Agrarian discontent was a factor which could lead peasants to reject the lead of their landlord, and to defy not only royalist but also parliamentarian landlords by remaining neutral or joining the other side. Thus class conflicts between peasants and landlords could operate for or against king or parliament.

Craftsmen and Capitalists

Parliament found strong bases of support in the manufacturing districts. At the outbreak of war there were strong upsurges of mass support for parliament in the clothmaking areas of Essex and Suffolk. David Underdown confirms that much of the strength of the parliamentarians in the southwest of England lay 'in the clothing districts of north Somerset and Wiltshire and in towns like Dorchester and Taunton'. In Devon most of the clothmaking regions and towns adhered to parliament. In Gloucestershire there would not have been a significant parliamentarian party without the backing of the cloth manufacturing districts (Underdown 1985: 170, 194–5, 203, 206–7, 276; Stoyle 1994: 155–6, 160–1; Rollison 1992: 148).

The clothmaking districts of the West Riding of Yorkshire, which were suffering from severe economic depression, provided the base for parliamentarianism in the county (Johnson 1848: vol. II: 367–72). The Saviles had identified themselves with the interests of the clothiers and clothmakers who, however, did not follow Lord Savile when he became a royalist in 1642, instead they looked to the Fairfaxes, who raised forces for parliament in the cloth manufacturing towns of the West Riding. 'I have hitherto supported this army', wrote Lord Fairfax, 'by the loans and contributions, for the most part, of the parishes of Leeds, Halifax, and Bradford, and some other small clothing towns adjacent, being the only well-affected people of the county' (Bell 1849: vol. I: 28–9). Their support for parliament had been stimulated by the fear of 'papists' which swept through the West Riding. John Hodgson, who lived near Halifax, heard that 'the parliament had declared their fears and jealousies, that there was a popish party about the king, carrying on a design to alter religion; that the war with Scotland was procured for to make way for it; that the rebellion in Ireland was framed in England, and should have been acted here' (Hodgson 1806: 95–6). Jonathan Priestley, a member of a West Riding family of clothiers, remembered:

... all trade and business was interrupted and laid aside, Lord Fairfax and Sir Thomas his son, came to Leeds and those parts to list soldiers; my brother Samuel went amongst the rest, but he came over to Goodgreave to take his leave of my mother, uncles, and friends. What entreaty and persuasions there was to keep him at home, but could not prevail. My mother went along with him a quarter of a mile, and I with her, as children use to do; she besought him with tears not to go; I remember his words, 'Mother', says he, 'pray be content; if I stay at home I can follow no employment, but be forced to hide myself in one hole or another, which I cannot endure; I had rather venture my life in the field, and, if I die, it is in a good cause'. So most honest men thought in those times, when hundreds of Protestants were daily murdered in Ireland, and fearing the same tragedy would be acted in England ... . (Priestly 1883: 26–7.)

The earl of Newcastle with a large royalist army entered Yorkshire from the north and drove Fairfax's army from Tadcaster to Selby, cutting it off from its base in the West Riding. Leeds surrendered. Many in Bradford thought resistance hopeless, but 'some religious persons in the parish, considering what danger might result both to their consciences and country from such cowardice and treachery', resolved to fight and 'invited all the well-affected in the parish to assist them'. All the soldiers of the militia, with their arms, and 'most of those who were fitted for service as volunteers', were with the Fairfaxes, from whom no help could be expected, and so for the defence of the town there were only 40 men with 'muskets and calivers', 30 with 'fowling, birding and smaller pieces', 'well nigh twice as many clubmen', and 'never a gentleman in the parish to command us'. As the royalist army approached on Sunday 18 December 1642 Bradford sent out appeals for help to the chapels of Halifax and Bingley, which responded, but few came with muskets and most had only clubs or 'scythes laid in poles'. Nevertheless the royalists were driven back and the defenders of Bradford passed the night on their guards 'telling what exploits had been done, and blessing God for his deliverance'. (Manning 1991: 80–1, 243, 262, 267, 298–305.)

Coventry was an important manufacturing and commercial centre. It had a population of around 7000 and its main business was spinning and weaving, finishing and marketing cloth. There were royalist and parliamentarian factions within the governing elite of the city but the majority of the corporation was uncommitted and tried not to offend either side. The parliamentarian faction, however, led by alderman John Barker, Member of Parliament for the city, got the upper hand because it had the greater popular support. Hundreds of citizens took arms for parliament, and hundreds more came to their support from nearby towns and villages, most notably from Birmingham. When Charles I came in person with armed men, Coventry refused to admit him and was held as an important garrison for parliament throughout the Civil War. Barker raised a regiment and its officers were small merchants and professional men, including two physicians and a feltmaker: 'these were men of some substance but not hitherto central figures in the city'. The ranks were filled with 'independent craftsmen, including weavers and tailors along with some labourers ...' (Hughes 1992a: 70, 79–80).

Birmingham was a rapidly growing manufacturing centre. From a population of no more than 1500 in the early sixteenth century, it had increased to probably about 5000 in the mid-seventeenth century. Nailmaking and cutlery were its main trades, which were more and more falling under the control of capitalists who dominated the production of raw materials and the marketing of finished products. Technological innovations brought higher productivity, increased capital investment, and more large-scale businesses. Ann Hughes describes the new type of society being formed:

> The Birmingham area underwent a great transformation in this period: new industrial methods and a greatly increased and mobile population produced a society very different from the more traditional rural areas. The local gentry, apart from leasing their land for mills, were not greatly involved in the iron industry; more typical were men who had made their own way in the world ... Birmingham had no resident lord of the manor from 1530 on, and in this relatively free society enterprising men found opportunities to make their fortunes in new ways and social relationships became increasingly based on commercial ties rather than deference and paternalism. This area, to contemporaries, was one where traditional loyalties seemed weaker. (Hughes 1987: 8–10.)

Birmingham was a centre of zeal for religious reformation and in the eyes of royalists 'a pestilent and seditious town', 'than whom his majesty has not found more malicious people in the whole course of this rebellion'. As well as sending 300 volunteers to assist Coventry, it contributed 100 men to defend Warwick castle. It supplied 15,000 swords to the parliament's army but would make none for the king's. Robert Porter's mill, which cost £100 to erect, manufactured swordblades 'only for the service of the parliament'. Birmingham, unlike Coventry, was not a walled town and it was not a defensible place, so when Prince Rupert approached with a royalist force of 2000 men in 1643, the minister and 'better sort' argued against resistance, but 'the middle and inferior sort of people' insisted that they stand firm. They had no horsemen and only 120 musketeers, but they kept Rupert at bay for almost an hour until overrun by his cavalry. Fourteen of the inhabitants of the town were killed, including three cutlers, two cobblers, a glazier, a labourer and two women. Porter described three of the dead as 'my honest workmen, whose lives I would I had redeemed with my estate'. The royalists plundered the town and took some £1000 in money and goods, and pulled down Porter's mill. They fired the town, destroying 87 houses and leaving 340 people homeless (Manning 1991: 286–92).

Not all the industrial areas supported parliament in the Civil War, not even all the clothmaking districts. The tin miners of Cornwall and Devon gave fervent support to the king and enabled the royalists to take control of the southwest of England. (Hutton 1982: 20–1; Underdown 1985: 203–4, 206–7; Hughes 1991: 144–5; Stoyle 1994: 16–18, 68–9, 90–1, 157–8, 160–1, 237.) But it remains the case that most clothmaking districts did give militant support to parliament, and historians agree that it was religion which made the difference between parliamentarian and royalist industrial areas. Commitment to radical reform of the church marked the parliamentarian clothmaking districts, demonstrating that the emergence of ideology, at this time religious ideology, led to radical political action.

David Underdown relates the division in the Civil War to different types of farming regions, but this is less plausible than to relate it to a distinction between wholly agrarian and partly industrialised districts (Morrill 1993: 224–41). It is, however, more complex than that, for within the latter there was a division between those which benefited from government regulation of the growing market economy and those which found such regulation irksome. During the 1630s the government had pursued with a new vigour, backed up by the court of star chamber, the long-established policy of economic regulation, in order to control prices and wages and to maintain standards in the processes of manufacture. In this it was supported by many merchants, especially in export trades, who were concerned to keep up the quality of goods, and by some manufacturers who suffered from the competition of shoddy goods. But at the same time there was resistance to government interference from many manufacturers who regarded it as hindering the expansion of production, especially in the cloth industry (Sharpe, Kevin 1992: 246–9). A contrast may be made between, for example, the royalism of the tin miners of Cornwall and Devon, whose livelihoods depended on privileges and protection from the crown, and the parliamentarianism of the clothmakers of Gloucestershire who resisted government inspectors and regulation of their industry. In manufacturing areas, opposition to the regime of Charles I was often aroused by a general dislike of outside intervention in their local affairs. Resentment against the interference of the central government, through the bishops, in the affairs of their parish church, as in the matter of the placing of the communion table, correlated with resistance to the attempts of the central government to impose and enforce controls over their industries.

Much cloth manufacture was located in rural rather than urban areas, and there was a considerable overlap between industry and agriculture: farmers engaged in spinning and weaving and many clothmakers had some land, but increasing numbers of them had little or none and approximated to an industrial proletariat. The latter were very poor at the best of times, but during the periodic depressions of trade and mass unemployment they came close to starving. They were the most turbulent and radical section of the population, and while it may be supposed that grinding poverty 'eroded their respect for traditional values and thus, by extension, for the system of government itself' (Stoyle 1994: 160), it is also the case that they looked to government to revive trade, keep them at work, stop their wages being reduced, and relieve their poverty (Sharp 1980: ch. 3). The struggles of clothworkers and their employers over wage-cuts and lay-offs meant that there was no certainty that they would take the same side in the Civil War (Rollison 1992: 157–61). But where animosities were masked by shared hostility towards the religious policies of the central government, and by common dislike for the aristocracy as an unproductive and parasitic class which lived off the labours of others, they did join their employers, men of the 'middling sort', and some few of the gentry who were engaged in the cloth industry or derived their income from tenants occupied in that industry, in the parliamentarian party, although it was an alliance fraught with ambivalence and latent antagonism.

Overseas Merchants and Domestic Traders

In the first detailed attempt to establish the allegiances of London merchants in the Civil War, Valerie Pearl found that most of the biggest merchants, who dominated the city government and the great export companies with royal charters of monopoly, were royalists, while the parliamentarians were 'merchants of the middle rank', '... wealthy, but not the wealthiest men in the city', '... important traders but not directors of the chartered companies' (Pearl 1961: 243–4, 276–7, 282–4). More recently Robert Brenner has examined 274 of the elite of London merchants. There is no evidence about the allegiances of more than half of them, but of the remaining 130, 78 were royalists, 43 were parliamentarians and nine changed sides. Breaking these down by companies, the leading merchants of the Levant and East India companies, who controlled the city government before 1642, were overwhelmingly royalists, while the Merchant Adventurers, who were less politically dominant than they had been in the sixteenth century, were more evenly divided (Brenner 1993: 375–88).

Keith Lindley in his analysis of party-forming London petitions of 1641–42 concludes that the royalist petitioners 'typified the men of wealth and superior standing, the city's traditional rulers, whose strong links with the pre-1640 regime, and instinctive caution and conservatism, made them natural opponents of the advocates of radical religious and political change'. Twice as many overseas merchants signed the royalist petition as signed the parliamentarian petitions. The typical signatory of the latter 'was the more modestly prosperous domestic tradesman with his own house and shop, and sometimes other city property, who was engaged in the retailing of textile and other goods'. He was a citizen of substance but 'generally less prosperous, well-connected and powerful' than the typical signatory of the royalist petition. 'It was this kind of London citizen, working with fellow militants in his parish, ward and livery company, and ready to exert a radical influence in the city's and kingdom's affairs, who provided much of the dynamic of the English Revolution' (Lindley 1992).

The great merchants were closely tied to the old monarchical-aristocratic economic and social order. They were involved in the exchange rather than the production of commodities, their profits depended on buying cheap and selling dear, and they sought and obtained royal and aristocratic favours to rig the market in their interest, such as through the monopolies of the great London overseas trading companies. They relied on their political power as the ruling elite of London to exploit the producers and to eliminate competition, and to increase and retain their wealth. They had no wish to subvert the old political and economic order, indeed they formed one of its main bulwarks. The king's cause was the defence of the existing social hierarchy, in which they were close to the top, and so they supported it, or did not oppose it. Their main aim was to defend their political and economic privileges. They were merchant capitalists but they were not instrumental in the development of capitalism in agricultural or industrial production.

While the big merchants engaged in trade with Europe, the Mediterranean and the East, through the monopoly companies, were predominantly royalists, there was a new branch of overseas trade that was different. Brenner demonstrates the role of colonisation in shaping the English Revolution. In contrast to commerce with Europe and Asia, trade with North America and the Caribbean depended upon first establishing and developing the production of tobacco and sugar: the crucial point is that in this area the merchants were engaged in production as well as trade.

Virginia (including Maryland) and the Caribbean Islands (including Bermuda) became the chief productive centres in British America. Before 1640 they produced mainly tobacco, which was shipped to England, and from there to the rest of Europe and the Near East. Between 1622 and 1638 imports from the American colonies to England rose from £61,000 to £2 million worth of tobacco a year. The men who provided the capital and entrepreneurship for colonial development did not come from the established elite of merchants in the chartered overseas trading companies. Some of them began by emigrating to the colonies and starting up plantations, from which they often used the profits to return to London and set up as overseas merchants, but continuing to be involved with the colonial economy. Others started as domestic traders, sea captains, or shopkeepers in London, and extended their business by exporting provisions to the colonies and importing tobacco. From a mass of small traders engaged in this commerce there emerged an elite which

> provided the most important source of motivation, capital, and organisation for the whole colonisation movement ... They were behind almost every important colonial adventure of the period and controlled a disproportionate share of the trade ... They dominated the rapidly developing tobacco trades with Virginia and the West Indies, which formed the heart of the new American commercial economy.

During the revolution sugar planting was introduced into the West Indies and was more profitable than tobacco. The elite group, which already dominated American enterprise, 'provided much of the energy and capital' behind this 'commercial-industrial development'. Tobacco was produced on small plots by white farmers but sugar was produced on large plantations by black slaves. The introduction of sugar 'opened the way for the decline of small-scale production, the replacement of free white by black slave labour, and the concentration of land and capital in the hands of a relatively small number of businessmen who could afford to invest and innovate' (Brenner 1993: 113–15, 154–62).

Brenner shows that the colonial merchants, or 'new merchants' as he calls them, were overwhelmingly parliamentarians in the Civil War. Of the small number of merchants in the Levant and East India companies who opted for parliament, most were also involved in the colonial trades with the Americas. Very few royalist merchants were active in the colonial trades (Brenner 1993: 375–88).

The correlation between the parliamentarian cause and overseas expansion and colonisation became intertwined with the fate of

Ireland. Following the rising of the Irish catholics in 1641, parliament (with the king's reluctant consent) offered 2.5 million acres of Irish land in return for investments to finance the reconquest of Ireland. Over £300,000 was thus raised and prominent amongst the investors were 'new merchants' involved in colonisation in North America and the Caribbean. They would be supporters of the revolution which led in the 1650s to the Cromwellian conquest of Ireland and confiscation of Irish land, which allowed them to realise their investment – Cromwell himself was one of the investors. Thus the subjection of Ireland belongs in the context of English overseas expansion and colonisation (Lindley 1994). English capitalism would advance in the English Revolution through the subjugation of the Irish and the enslavement of blacks.

The social and economic contexts of the 'new merchants' lends support to the identification of the parliamentarian party with 'middle sort of people'. Many of them were the younger sons of minor gentry or prosperous yeomen, and some came from commercial families in provincial towns. They began as domestic traders, shopkeepers and ship captains, and many of them combined colonial trade with domestic trade from their London shops. Thus by their social origins and 'their continuing participation in domestic commercial activities' they had 'strong and extensive ties' with the middle layer of London's population – shopkeepers, mariners, craftsmen – and 'could, in fact, in 1640, be properly regarded as belonging to that layer' (Brenner 1993: 114, 159, 184, 395). Brenner describes the parliamentarian party in London as follows:

> ... rank-and-file citizens drawn heavily from among shop-keepers, mariners, artisans, and craftsmen, with new merchants making up one (though only one) crucial element of its leadership ... These men were largely cut off from the sources of commercial, political, and ecclesiastical power by the privileged merchant companies that controlled much of foreign trade, by the aldermanic oligarchy that dominated city government, and by the crown and the ecclesiastical hierarchy, which exerted a stranglehold over the official parish churches of London. They were, in consequence, open to religio-political courses of action ...

They shifted the parliamentarian cause in the capital in 1641–42 to a struggle to revolutionise the city's government by reducing the power of the aldermen and increasing that of the more represen-tative common council, and to revolutionise ecclesiastical government by replacing episcopacy with greater local control over their parish churches and ministers, either through a Presbyterian or Congregational form of organisation. This was a political conflict with social connotations, because the conservative forces drew their strength from privileged merchants of the overseas trading companies, and the radical forces drew their strength from domestic traders and craftsmen (Brenner 1993: 693).

One of the crucial issues was the conflict of domestic traders and craftsmen with overseas merchants. The aim of the chartered companies was to restrict the numbers engaged in overseas commerce and to keep out shopkeepers and small producers. Company charters confined overseas trade to 'mere merchants' and excluded retailers and craftsmen. There were conflicts when the latter intruded illegally into the companies' trades. This helps to explain the parliamentarianism and radicalism of many shopkeepers and craftsmen in London, and after the Civil War, their support for the Leveller movement, which campaigned persistently against the monopoly companies and for the opening of overseas trade to all who had the desire and the resources to participate.

This also applies to provincial centres, where David Sacks shows that at Bristol for at least a century before the revolution there was controversy over the claim of the city's major overseas merchants to an exclusive right to trade with foreign markets. The Society of Merchant Venturers of Bristol excluded retailers and craftsmen from overseas trade. By 1640 there was a long history of antagonism between the Merchant Venturers and the retailers and craftsmen, whose aim was that all citizens should be free to engage in overseas trade if they wished. It became one of the bases of the division into parties in the Civil War, when, as a contemporary observer maintained, the king's cause in Bristol was favoured by 'the wealthy and powerful men ... but disgusted by the middle rank ...'. This is confirmed by Sacks, who says that '... the majority of Bristol's merchants conceived of themselves in the king's party when events forced them, sometimes against their wills, to decide where they stood'; while '... many of the most ardent supporters of the parliamentary cause during the civil wars came from the ranks of the city's shopkeepers and craftsmen'.

> The rapid rise of colonial enterprise in the 1640s and 1650s ... provided new openings for small shopkeepers and artisans to enter into overseas commerce. In the early 1650s, hundreds of townsmen ... engaged freely in dealings with the Chesapeake region and the West Indies, shipping small wares and indentured servants in return for the tobacco and sugar their overseas customers produced. A number of these figures had a history of political support for parliament and ... many too were members of the sects. (Sacks 1992.)

The exclusion of shopkeepers and craftsmen from engaging in the profession of a merchant not only maximised the profits of the latter, but also upheld the concept of hierarchy, which as it separated the superior status and function of the gentlemen from all below them, so it elevated the status and function of merchants above those of shopkeepers and craftsmen. Challenge to the ecclesiastical hierarchy by 'middle sort' radicals – the demand for the abolition of episcopacy – correlated with this challenge to the secular hierarchy: they saw rights as being located in the community as a whole rather than in people with a particular status or function; and as the radicals regarded liberty of conscience as a natural right, so they regarded liberty to trade as a natural right. After the Civil War the Levellers said that it was the 'birthright' of 'every English native' who has goods, wares and merchandise 'to transport the same to any place beyond the seas, and there to convert them to his own profit'. They argued that it was contrary to the native rights of Englishmen and to the fundamental laws of the land to prevent a man from trading to certain parts of the world unless he belonged to a company (Manning 1991: 388–90).

There was a strong thrust by the revolutionaries for the opening of commerce to more traders. This, they believed, would stimulate economic growth by widening existing markets, developing new ones, and encouraging the production of more commodities and goods. They argued that, while more competition might hurt the wealthiest merchants, the total volume of trade would increase, although spread among more individuals, and the total profits would be greater, although dispersed more widely. It was a viewpoint which combined economic growth with less inequality in the distribution of wealth, at least for the 'middling sort'. A tract of 1645 said: 'The strength of a kingdom consists in the riches of many subjects, not of a few ...', which is 'why there are fewer beggars seen in commonwealths [i.e. republics] than in kingdoms, because of community and freedom of trading, by which means the wealth of the land is more equally distributed amongst the natives' (Appleby 1978: 109–16, 127).

'Middle Sort of People' and the Aristocracy

Three very well-known contemporary accounts of the parties in the Civil War by parliamentarians reflect their experiences and their perceptions of their own party. According to Lucy Hutchinson, wife of the parliamentarian commander at Nottingham: '... most of the gentry of the county were disaffected to the parliament; most of the middle sort, the able substantial freeholders, and other commons, who had not their dependence upon the malignant nobility and gentry, adhered to the parliament' (Hutchinson 1885: vol. I: 141). Richard Baxter, minister at Kidderminster in Worcestershire, wrote: 'On the parliament's side were ... the smaller part (as some thought) of the gentry in most of the counties, and the greatest part of the tradesmen, and freeholders, and the middle sort of men; especially in those corporations and counties which depend on clothing and such manufactures'. Baxter was familiar with the latter because '... the town lives upon the weaving of Kidderminster stuffs ...' (Sylvester 1696: 30, 89). John Corbet, a minister of Gloucester and also acquainted with clothmaking districts, maintained that support for parliament, besides 'some gleanings of the gentry', came from 'the yeomen, farmers, clothiers, and the whole middle rank of the people ...', including 'such as use manufactures' (Washbourn 1823: vol. I: 9, 16). Corbet's analysis is supported by modern research (Rollison 1992: ch. 6; Sacks 1992: 109–13). A significant feature of these accounts is that they adopt the new terminology of social analysis by speaking of 'middle sort' and 'middling rank', indicating awareness of a distinctive grouping in society, with a capacity to act independently of the aristocracy and to assert itself in national affairs. Ann Hughes finds that in Warwickshire support for parliament came from 'men of middling wealth' in the north of the county – 'lesser gentry', 'independent freeholders', 'enterprising small landholders', and 'industrial craftsmen'. She thinks this is 'typical of the areas where parliament obtained support in 1642' – '... industrial and pastoral areas where independent and prosperous freeholders were numerous'. (Hughes 1987: 149–55, 161–2, 169, 179, 196–7, 228; 1989: 243–7.)

The king directed his appeals to the aristocracy but parliament wooed the 'middle sort'. A pamphlet – *The Moderator expecting sudden peace or certain ruin* (1643) – alleged: 'It has been observed, the parliament has made little difference (or not the right) between the gentry and yeomanry, rather complying and winning upon the latter, than regarding or applying themselves at all to the former.' 'Middle sort' parliamentarians were influenced by arguments that the king was bent upon making himself an absolute monarch and was a party to a conspiracy to introduce 'popery' into the church. They became suspicious of peers and greater gentry when they saw so many of them supported the king. When Charles summoned the gentry of Yorkshire to meet him at York in May 1642 '... to advise with him in some particulars concerning the honour and safety of his majesty's person, and the well-being and peace of this our county ...', 'divers thousands of freeholders' protested at not being invited, 'conceiving ourselves according to the proportions of our estates equally interested in the common good of the county' and of the nation. Many of the freeholders went to York but the doors of the meeting place were shut against them, and they conceived themselves 'abundantly injured' and said they would not be bound by decisions taken without their consent (Campbell 1960: 356–7).

When the king 'borrowed' the arms of the militia the two houses of parliament accused him of practising one of 'the most mischievous principles of tyranny ... that ever were invented, that is to disarm the middle sort of people, who are the body of the kingdom'. A parliamentarian tract – *A Sovereign Salve to cure the blind* (1643) – claimed that this was proof that the royalists intended 'a government at discretion' after the French fashion, because 'the middle sort of people of England, and yeomanry' were the chief obstacles to such a change, and as they composed the main part of the militia, 'then by policy, or even plain force' they must be disarmed:

> whereby from being in the happiest condition of any of their rank perhaps in Europe, nay in the world (who here live like men, and are wont to fight or die like men in honour or defence of their country) might well be reduced to the terms of the peasants of France, of villeinage and slavery ...

The author dismissed 'the scum of the people' as being incapable of understanding this or caring about it.

Jeremiah Burroughes, a prominent preacher in the parliamentarian cause, declared in a sermon, *The Glorious Name of God*, printed in 1643:

> Would you know why so many of the gentry in most counties throughout the kingdom are so malignant? ... Many of them had rather enslave themselves and their posterities to those above them, than not to have their wills upon those that are under them; they would fain bring it to be with us as it is in France, that the gentry should be under the nobility and courtiers, and all the country people, the peasants, be under them as slaves, they live in miserable bondage under the gentry there, who generally are cavaliers. There is no country in the world, where countrymen, such as we call the yeomanry, yea, and their farmers and workmen under them, do live in that fashion and freedom as they do in England, in all other places they are slaves in comparison, their lives are so miserable as they are not worth the enjoying, they have no influence at all into the government they are under, nothing to do in the making of laws, or any way consenting to them, but must receive them from others, according to their pleasure; but in England every freeholder has an influence into the making and consenting every law he is under [he has a vote in elections to parliament], and enjoys his own with as true a title as the nobleman enjoys whatsoever is his. This freedom many of the proud gentry are vexed at ...

It is notable that Burroughes focused upon the yeomen and freeholders rather than upon small tenant farmers or labourers.

The foremost parliamentarian newspaper, *Mercurius Britanicus*, answered a slur in the chief royalist newspaper, *Mercurius Aulicus*, that the committee which ran the war effort for parliament in Hertfordshire was a 'yeoman committee':

> This is it which 'goes against the hair' with them at Oxford [the king's headquarters]; they have a plot in hand to enslave the whole commons of the kingdom, and therefore cannot endure to hear that the yeomanry should be held of any esteem, or have anything to do in matters of the least public concernment. It was the old court-plot, ever to hoist up the prerogative of the king, and suppress the liberty of the subject; setting before his eyes the absolute power of France as a pattern of emulation, so that in time the ancient and free English title of yeoman should have been changed into that of peasant or slave; and so our whole estates and liberties been made a sacrifice to the avarice and flattery of courtiers.

Royalist propaganda constantly asserted that the king's cause was supported by men of the highest birth and best fortunes, and that the parliamentarians were men of low birth and mean fortunes, even 'the rabble'. Parliamentarians did not attempt to counter this by claiming that they had the support of some peers and greater gentry, rather they denied that their supporters were the poorest and basest of the people, and insisted on the respectability of their party as consisting mainly of 'the middle sort of people' (Malcolm 1983: 157, 162–3). This is no proof that the parliamentarian party was so composed, but it does show that many parliamentarians were conscious that the existence of a substantial middle rank of people made society and politics in England different from the continent, and perceived that political freedom and Protestant religion ultimately rested on that difference (Wootton 1990: 667).

Most historians deny that the English Civil War was a class struggle. Either they maintain that there were no classes in early modern society, only status, occupational and interest groups, or, if there were classes, they lacked class consciousness. They point out that every strata or group was divided by the conflict and that both parties were broad cross-sections of society: there were royalists as well as parliamentarians amongst the 'middle sort'. (Morrill 1993: 214–23; Underdown 1985: 2–4, 168–71, 192–201, 204–7, 277–8.) Most historians also tend to harp on both parties being small minorities, with each being driven by even smaller numbers of committed partisans or extremists. But as the same historians see the conflict as being primarily about religion, there is a contradiction between the stress on the smallness of the parties and the emphasis on the capacity of religious issues to move large numbers of people, whether for or against further reforms of the church, or

by fear of 'papists' or 'sectaries'. It is not plausible that a country
could be plunged into two decades of turmoil, upheaval and violent
conflicts, without divisions running wide and deep, and active
partisans on both sides would soon have been contained and neu-
tralised if they had not been nourished by very large numbers of
less active people who in varying degrees sympathised with their
causes. In no conflict in history do all, or even a majority, of one
class line up on one side and all, or even a majority, of another class
on the other; and in no conflict are there only members of one class
on each side. Whether or not a conflict is a class conflict depends
on the extent to which it involves class issues. In the English Civil
War the reality behind the social diversity of each party was revealed
by differences of ethos: an aristocratic ethos dominated the royalist
party however many plebeians it contained, and a 'middle sort' ethos
began to drive forward the parliamentarian party, even though it
contained some aristocrats, and indeed was led by them nationally.
The parliamentarian party was suffused with anti-aristocratic
feelings even though it was led by aristocrats, and indeed partly
against their leadership. These feelings distinguished those of the
'middle sort' who became parliamentarians from those who remained
neutral or joined the royalists, and the former had more influence
than the latter over ensuing events.

The 'middle sort of people' were based in the class of independent small producers, but some of these were rising into capitalist
employers and others were declining into wage-earning employees.
Classes are constantly being shaped and reshaped, a process out
of which history itself is made. A whole class does not become radicalised or class conscious at once, and the 'middle sort' in general
lacked the coherence to take a single class position. Groups become
conscious of themselves as a class in the course of conflict with other
groups identifiable as different classes. Out of the diversity of the
'middle sort' there emerged elements that, without being exactly
the same as the growing capitalist or bourgeois tendency, became
conscious of the difference between their economic and ideological position and that of others, and found themselves united to defend
it against the party which they identified with the aristocracy or ruling
class. Thus they reached a level of both radicalism and class consciousness. Just as royalists saw themselves as defending the
aristocracy, even though all aristocrats did not join them, so parliamentarians saw themselves as defending the 'middle sort', even
though all the 'middle sort' did not unite with them. A revolutionary
struggle is a class struggle and so this development within the
'middle sort' converted the English Civil War into a revolutionary
struggle.

Statements by parliamentarians are not to be taken as evidence
for the motives of royalists, but they may be taken as evidence of

how some parliamentarians perceived the nature of the conflict. 'Most men ... did undoubtedly foresee greater hopes of liberty from the parliament than the king's party ...', wrote John Corbet, who alleged, in emotive language, that the nobles and powerful gentry who sided with the king did so from 'a desire of vast dominion, dignity, revenge, or rapine', and out of 'an hatred of the commons, and a strong disposition to the ends of tyranny', caring not 'to render themselves the slaves of princes, that they also might rule over their neighbours as vassals' (Washbourn 1823: vol. I: 8–9, 16–17). Edmund Ludlow, a radical squire and parliamentarian commander in Wiltshire, held that 'many of the nobility and gentry were contented to serve the king's arbitrary designs, if they might have leave to insult over such as were of a lower order ...' (Ludlow 1894: vol. I: 96).

The royalist nobility and greater gentry allegedly resented the wealth and status which some people of the 'middle sort' were acquiring. The yeomen, farmers and clothiers of Gloucestershire, wrote Corbet, were

> a generation of men truly laborious, jealous of their properties, whose principal aim is liberty and plenty, and whilst in an equal rank with their neighbours they desire only not to be oppressed, and account themselves extremely bound to the world, if they may keep their own; such therefore continually thwart the intentions of tyranny ...

They became parliamentarians because they felt threatened by the royalist nobility and greater gentry, who detested 'a close, hardy, and industrious way of living ...' (Washbourn 1823: vol. I: 8–9). David Rollison argues that the conflict in Gloucestershire, which surfaced in the parliamentary elections of 1640 and shaped the parties of the Civil War in the county, was based on 'long-standing and deeply rooted social divisions' between, on the one side, 'a class of magnates with neo-feudal (or "absolutist") pretensions', and on the other side, the people of the mercantile and manufacturing districts. The magnate class regarded themselves as an 'inherently superior caste', based on values 'embedded, by long practice and by the continuous re-invention of traditions, in the feudal past'. This 'coterie of magnate households' was mostly situated in northwest Gloucestershire and focused on the household of the Brydges, lords Chandos of Sudely, self-styled 'kings of the Cotswolds'. They sought to reassert their old domination of the county and found an obstacle to this in the political independence and initiative gained by the 'middle sort' of the clothmaking valleys of Stroudwater in central Gloucestershire (Rollison 1992: 146–8). The attempt by Lord Chandos to implement the king's commission of array was frustrated by a popular uprising in Cirencester and the clothmaking districts, as described in Chapter 3.

John Ashe, of whom there is an account in Chapter 1, the very wealthy clothier and parliamentarian leader in Somerset, publicised in *A Memento for Yeomen, Merchants, Citizens, and all the Commons in England* (1642) a story about Lord Poulett, who prominently supported the effort of the marquis of Hertford to secure the west for the king in 1642:

> It is really reported by the mouths of those who were eye and ear witnesses, that my lord Poulett in opposition to the militia at a combustion at Wells, with many imprecatious oaths and execrations (in the height of fury) declared, that it was not fit for any yeoman to have allowed him from his own labours, any more than the poor moiety of £10 a year, and withall manifested to this purpose, though not perhaps in these words, that when the power should be totally on their side, they shall be compelled to live at that low allowance, notwithstanding their estates are gotten with a great deal of labour and industry ...

Whether it was true or not, the story seemed plausible enough to the 'middle sort' of Somerset, who took it as directed not only against yeomen but also against tradesmen and merchants. It was said that it was one of the reasons for the popular uprising against the marquis of Hertford and his party, people believing that if the royalists triumphed 'all should be, upon the matter, no better than slaves to the lords', and that there was no other way to protect themselves from this and to preserve their estates and liberties than by adhering to parliament. When the royalist earl of Derby was repulsed from Manchester by the parliamentarians of southeast Lancashire, a Mancunian declared: 'O England's yeomen and husbandmen look to yourselves, for if you stand not to it, as we of Manchester do, but be overcome, look for ever to be slaves, for you see how this bloody tyrant [the earl of Derby] rages ...'. 'If the nobility and gentry of the kingdom still go on to make the commons of England, gentle slaves in their religion and liberty, they themselves, that is so many of them as run these courses, may happen to be taken before they die, at least in esteem inferior to commons' (Manning 1991: 263–4, 327).

Henry Parker, the important parliamentarian propagandist, declared in *The Oath of Pacification* (1643):

> That there are more lords and great ones, bishops, judges, etc. with them, than on the parliament's side, I deny not ... We all know, that the apostle says, 1. *Cor.1.26* 'Not many wise men after the flesh, not many mighty men, not many noble, but God has chosen the poor of this world'; and our blessed saviour,

Matth. 11. 25 'You have hid these things from the wise, and prudent, and revealed them to babes', poor mechanical men. *John 7. 48, 49* 'Do any of the rulers, or of the pharisees, believe on him?' The scribes and pharisees, great rabbis and doctors of the law, who of all others, should have been the greatest furtherers of the Gospel, and friends to Christ, were the greatest enemies, and most bitter opposers of both, and most woefully blinded in spiritual and saving truths of God. The great men and worldly wisemen, generally in all ages have been most corrupt, and no friends to Christ and reformation, *Nehem. 5. 7* 'I rebuked the nobles, and the rulers and I set a great assembly against them', *Chap. 13. 11* I contended with the rulers, *Vers. 17* I contended with the nobles; the commons generally stood right for reformation, and were freest from the sins of the times, but the nobles, and great ones were so faulty and corrupt, that good Nehemiah was constrained to make a great party of the commons to oppose them ...

It was a constant theme of the sermons of parliamentarian clergy that God, from the beginnings of Christianity to the Reformation and the present times, worked through 'the poorer and meaner sort of people': 'few of the princes and nobles putting their necks to the work of the Lord', declared Stephen Marshall in *The Song of Moses* (1643); 'not many mighty, not many noble are called ... poor Lazarus goes to heaven when rich Dives is carried to hell', pronounced Edmund Calamy in *The Nobleman's Pattern of true and real thankfulness* (1643). Such statements boosted the morale of ordinary parliamentarians. The 'godly' among them were encouraged to shed their customary deference towards the king and the aristocracy, and infused with a sense of their own superior worth and exalted mission. Some contemporaries discerned that social conflicts underlay religious differences, which would make 'little noise or disturbance in the world' but for association with social divisions which were 'the bitter root of all our breaches', as William Sprigge argued from the viewpoint of 1659 in a pamphlet *A Modest Plea for an Equal Commonwealth against Monarchy*: 'Were there not one interest of the nobility, another of the commonalty; one of the clergy, another of the laity; one of the lawyer, another of the countryman ... These are the interests that clash so much one against another, and make such tumults in the world ...'.

Jeremiah Burroughes enunciated four war aims that may be taken as reflecting the objectives of the 'middle sort' who supported parliament: that their property should be their own and not 'wholly at the will of another' (implying opposition to any arbitrary power and to taxation without the consent of parliament); that they should be subject only to such government as rested on the consent of the people; that their rights should be rooted in law and justice and not dependent on the grace or favour of great men, and that their consciences should be bound by no man but only by God (Wootton 1990: 667). This last point underpinned the other three, for all asserted the autonomy of the individual.

A broad concept of 'godliness' (a self-identifying quality which a 'godly' person could recognise that others either did or did not possess) defined and united a wide range of parliamentarians across doctrinal and organisational differences – Presbyterians, Congregationalists, Baptists. But amongst the 'godly' the more radical were distinguished by their rejection of a national established state church, whether episcopalian or Presbyterian. They formed independent and autonomous congregations, separate from the state church, in order to worship God according to the light of their individual consciences, which occasioned them to fragment into numerous sects. These sects, such as various sorts of Congregationalists and Baptists, formed a hard core of the parliamentarian party. Their membership had a social focus, for while it included some minor gentry, well-to-do yeoman farmers, and prosperous merchants and manufacturers, it consisted predominantly of small traders and craftsmen (McGregor and Reay 1984: 18–19, 35–7).

Oliver Cromwell recruited 'godly men', including many from the sects ('sectaries'), into his regiment in parliament's army, and he sought to appoint officers for their commitment to the cause irrespective of their social rank or precise form of 'godliness'. In a famous letter he defended the choice of Ralph Margery to be a captain though he was not a gentleman:

> I beseech you be careful what captains of horse you choose … If you choose godly honest men to be captains of horse, honest men will follow them … I had rather have a plain russet-coated captain that knows what he fights for, and loves what he knows, than that which you call a gentleman and is nothing else.

Cromwell was close to such 'plain men'. John Morrill shows that although he was born into the gentry and educated as a gentleman, and connected with the aristocracy, he inherited probably no more than £100 a year. In the early 1630s he was essentially 'a yeoman, a working farmer'. By 1641 his income was probably £300 a year (Morrill 1993: ch. 6).

Despite his connections with ancient riches, Cromwell's economic status was much closer to that of the 'middling sort' and urban merchants than to that of the county gentry and governors. He always lived in towns, not in a country manor house; and he worked for his living. He held no important local offices and had no tenants or others dependent upon him beyond a few household servants.

When he urged the appointment of 'russet-coated captains' '... this was not the condescension of a radical member of the elite, but the pleas of a man on the margins of the gentry on behalf of those with whom he had had social discourse and daily communion for twenty years' (Morrill: 1993: ch. 6). Cromwell gave leadership in the Civil War to a broad front of 'godly people' from the 'middling sort'.

End of the Aristocrats' War

The war could not be won by localised popular insurrections but only by a trained and disciplined national army. Initially parliament followed tradition and relied heavily on peers to command its forces. The incompetence of many of them as military commanders became increasingly evident, and most of them fought the war defensively and sought to end it by negotiation and compromise rather than by outright military victory, believing that the latter would lead to a more extreme constitutional and religious settlement of the conflict than they desired, and permit anti-aristocratic elements to gain further ground. Military setbacks and prolongation of the war led the House of Commons in 1644–45 to reorganise its armies. The Self-Denying Ordinance required members of both houses of parliament to resign from military commands. This got rid of the old aristocratic generals – notably the earls of Essex and Manchester – and allowed the formation of a new army – the New Model Army – under the command of Sir Thomas Fairfax and Oliver Cromwell, which became the instrument of outright victory for parliament in 1645–46. The House of Lords objected that this deprived the peers 'of that honour which in all ages has been given to them ... to be employed in military commands', and went against 'the constant practice' of England that the peers held the 'places of chiefest trust and command'. The Lords were overborne but the House of Commons felt it necessary to deny that its aim was to overthrow the peerage: it declared that it would preserve 'the rights and privileges belonging to the House of Peers ... and the right and honour belonging to the places and persons of the peers of England'. Sir John Evelyn, bringing this message to the Lords, said that one thing above all must reassure them that the Commons did not seek to overthrow the peerage, and this was 'that they that sit in the House of Commons are gentlemen'. The Lords were heartened by this and replied that 'notwithstanding some discourses that pass frequently about this town, they would never suspect the House of Commons, composed of so many gentlemen of ancient families, would do any act to the prejudice of the nobility of England'.

(Firth 1910: 143–51; Kishlansky 1979: 27, 34, 39; Adamson 1990: 109–20.) It was, however, a decisive moment: the army which became the instrument of victory was different from previous armies; it was one in which promotion was determined increasingly by professional merit rather than social rank; in which there was a leaven of ideological commitment to the cause; and in which 'middling sort' and plebeian elements gained voices in the affairs of the nation.

CHAPTER 5

The Other War

> ... the other war, fought between the partisans of both causes
> and the bulk of the population ...
>
> RONALD HUTTON, 1982

In proportion to the size of the population more Englishmen died
as a result of the Civil War in the seventeenth century than of either
of the world wars in the twentieth century: it was 'the bloodiest
conflict in relative terms in English history' (Carlton 1994: ch. 9).
Many people at the time asked: 'For what?'. Consideration should
now be given to those who did not support either side in the Civil
War, and the limits of popular attachment to parliament.

A royalist tract – *An Answer to a Seditious Pamphlet Entitled, Plain
English*, published at Oxford early in 1643 – made shrewd points
to counteract the popular appeal of the parliamentarians:

> I must plainly tell you, there never was any civil war, wherein
> the good of the people was not more cried up, and yet least
> intended. For assure yourselves, the interests of discontented
> nobles, or Members of Parliament, that have gained a greater
> power in your affections, are not the same with you of lower
> rank, and therefore they do but abuse you, and make you with
> hazard of your estates, and lives, and souls, cut out way to their
> ends.

The common people will waste their estates, beggar their wives and
children, and risk their lives 'to turn out old officers, and put new
in their places ... yet the kingdom will find a change in the persons
only, not in the justice ...'. The author recognised that zeal for
religious reformation had some popular appeal, and so he contended
that it was merely a cloak for the ambition of the parliamentarian
leaders to win power and 'to prefer themselves to the greatest
commands'. They countenanced 'schism in the church' and all kinds
of radical religious sects in order to use 'the godly' in their struggle
for power. Once they had achieved that, they would disappoint the
hopes of the religious reformers, who in any case could agree only
in overthrowing the existing church, but not on what to put in its
place. Thus he played the strongest royalist card by appealing to
the widespread popular attachment to the traditional church.

The mass of the people were engaged as ever in the daily struggle for the barest of livelihoods, and the war made that even more difficult. They were faced with conscription into one or other of the armies, and the likelihood of death from battle or disease; with lodging and feeding the soldiers of both sides without being paid (known as 'free-quarter'); with vastly increased taxation, even of the poor; with seizure of their horses, carts, crops, and with plunder of their money and goods, by both parties. A speedy end to the war seemed to many of them a greater and more immediate good than the cause of either side.

In 1644–45 there were popular uprisings against conscription and taxation in both royalist and parliamentarian quarters. In west Sussex the parliamentarians were in control and the revolt was directed against their administration.

> We can neither raise men or monies for Sir Thomas Fairfax's army, or upon any other ordinance, they not suffering our officers to impress [i.e. conscript], or when impressed taking them away by violence, sending sometimes a constable or tithingman with the blood running about his ears ... And in no better case are we for monies, it being one of their articles to pay such taxes only as they please, the fruits whereof we are too sensible of, not an £100 – though above £4000 due – being brought in since their first rising, no collector daring to distrain for fear of having his brains dashed out, forty servants and women rising together armed with prongs and other weapons ... (Fletcher 1975: 271–6.)

Herefordshire was a county dominated by the royalists, but early in 1645 country people in the Hundred of Broxash began to band together to resist taxes and conscription, seizures of their crops, and violence by soldiers from the royalist garrisons of Hereford and Canon Frome. They drove off soldiers gathering provisions for Hereford, whose governor sent out a punitive expedition which dispersed the crowds, killing some and taking others prisoner. This provoked a mass uprising and on 19 March 1645 thousands of peasants, some armed with muskets and the rest with clubs, marched on Hereford and besieged it for several days. They were led by 'men of moderate wealth and status'. Their demands were compensation for the widows and children of those slain, release of the prisoners, and withdrawal of all garrisons from the county. The governor of Hereford persuaded them to disperse by agreeing to pay compensation, free the prisoners, and remit one month's taxation. But he never intended to keep his promises, merely playing for time until the arrival of reinforcements extinguished the revolt (Hutton 1982: 163–4, 170; Gladwish 1985).

Historians have usually included such revolts in the movement known as the 'risings of the clubmen'. It is true this movement was occasioned by the same grievances of the country people against being conscripted, taxed, plundered, but it was distinguished by the politicisation of those grievances into an organised and sustained campaign to form local associations to defend themselves against plundering soldiers, to maintain neutrality between the two sides and to petition king and parliament for peace. The term 'clubmen' had two meanings, referring to poor peasants whose only weapons were clubs, but in this case to people who formed clubs or associations, and the 'clubmen' called themselves 'associates'. 'Risings of the clubmen' took place mainly in parts of Wiltshire, Dorset and Somerset, and to a less well-developed extent in parts of Worcestershire and Berkshire, but not so widely as historians have maintained. (Morrill 1967: 98–111; Underdown 1979 and 1980.)

Thousands attended great meetings at Gussage in Dorset on 25 May 1645, at Badbury Rings in Dorset on 28 May, and at Grovely in Wiltshire on 6 June. They resolved 'to join with and assist one another in the mutual defence of our laws, liberties, and posterities against all plunderers, and all other unlawful violence whatsoever'. They set up an organisation to maintain watches for any soldiers engaging in plunder or violence and to raise the associates in arms to stop and arrest such offenders. They also resolved 'that whatsoever person, though seemingly associated himself, shall be found to occasion any outcry or by other means to assemble any in favour or opposition to either party, king or parliament ... he shall be accounted unworthy of our protection as dissembling his inclination to our party, in frustrating according to his power our real intentions ...'. Wiltshire and Dorset collaborated closely and published their joint *Desires and Resolutions* (1645):

> We the miserable inhabitants of the said counties, being too deeply touched with the apprehension and sense of our past and present sufferings, occasioned only by these civil and unnatural wars within this kingdom; and finding by sad experience that, by means thereof, the true worship of almighty God and our religion are almost forgotten; and that our ancient laws and liberties (contrary to the Great Charter of England and the Petition of Right) are altogether swallowed up in the arbitrary power of the sword; and foreseeing that destruction, famine, and utter desolation will inevitably fall upon us, our wives, and children, unless God of his infinite mercy shall upon our true humiliation be graciously pleased to impose a period to these sad distractions, are unanimously resolved ... to join in petitioning his majesty, and the two houses of parliament for a happy peace, and accommodation of the present differences, without

further effusion of Christian blood; without which accommo-
dation we cannot expect the enjoyment of our religion, liberties,
or properties ...

On 24 June a great meeting at Sturminster Newton approved the
petitions to the king and the two Houses of parliament 'from the
distressed Protestants of Dorset and Wiltshire'. They justified their
assemblies as being 'to unite themselves as ... they humbly conceive
they lawfully may do, for the maintenance of their religion, laws,
liberties, and properties, against all unlawful violence and plundering
whatsoever ...'. They protested that justice had broken down and
the laws were no longer enforced, and that the 'immeasurable
taxes, continual free-quarter, and incessant plunderings' had
'scarcely left your suppliants sufficient for the support of life'.
They appealed for the renewal of negotiations between the king
and the two Houses for peace.

A parallel movement was taking place at the same time in
Somerset, where the clubmen declared in their petition to the king
and the two Houses that they were assembled because of 'intolerable slavery, under a most insolent soldiery', and of impoverishment
by 'endless contributions and plunders'. They were drawn together
'... not for sedition, but for the public peace, and in order thereunto,
to meet together in this our humble petition unto your excellent
majesty, and the said honourable Lords and Commons, and to put
ourselves into a general readiness, at the cry of the country, to pursue
and arrest all robbers and murderers, and all other felons, under
whose continual oppressions we could no longer endure'. They
complained of the breakdown of law and order, and of 'the cursed
sacrileges done upon holy places devoted to God's service' and 'the
grievous persecutions of reverend ministers ...'.

> We the gentlemen, freeholders, and others, all Protestants, and
> peaceable subjects of the county of Somerset, beholding with
> unexpressible affliction of our souls the many and terrible
> shakings of that well-built state of England ... are most humble
> suitors to your sacred majesty, and to the said honourable
> Lords and Commons, that our so long and much tottering
> kingdom may speedily be reposed upon her firm foundation,
> which we conceive to be the full and free convening in parliament,
> of your majesty's royal person, and of all the Lords, together
> with the Commons, as well them which have been heretofore
> duly elected to this parliament, and do yet survive, as others who
> ought to be so elected thither, to fill all places in it void by death ...

They praised a parliament, when properly composed of the king
as well as the two Houses, as being 'the most glorious body that is
visible in England', and they petitioned the two sides to appoint

commissioners 'to meet, treat, and agree of time and place, when
and where your majesty shall be, with your Houses of Lords and
Commons, both of them in their beautiful fullness of all their
members ...' (that meant the royalists being restored to their places
at Westminster).

The revolt of the clubmen was extinguished by the arrival in the
west of parliament's reorganised army, the New Model, under the
command of Sir Thomas Fairfax. On entering Somerset it found
2000 clubmen assembled on Knowle Hill, two miles from
Bridgwater, under banners inscribed 'Beati Pacifici' and 'For
Ourselves'. Fairfax and his officers went to meet them and asked
the cause of their assembly. Their leader, Humphrey Willis (of
yeoman stock rising into the gentry), replied that it was to preserve
their goods and to obtain peace, and showed copies of their petitions
to the king and parliament. Fairfax assured them that they would
not be plundered by his men, who would pay for what they had
from them. This proved enough to satisfy the peasants, who
dispersed and 'dropped away home by six and eight, ten or twenty
together, shooting off their guns ... in a way of triumph, for joy at
that news, that they should not be plundered ...' (Underdown 1973:
98–100, 105–8).

The clubmen of Dorset and Wiltshire, however, were less easily
placated and Fairfax arrested 50 of their leaders who were meeting
at Shaftesbury. The people rose to defend themselves and to secure
the release of their leaders. A large group assembled on Duncliffe
Hill, two miles from Shaftesbury, but confronted by Cromwell with
a thousand dragoons they were persuaded to disperse peacefully.
Several thousand more clubmen were gathered on Hambledon Hill,
behind the ancient earthworks which had protected their ancestors,
six miles from Shaftesbury. Fairfax's chaplain, Edward Bowles,
recounted in a newsletter from the army that at the foot of the hill
Cromwell's force met a lone peasant armed with a musket:

> ... asked whither he was going? He said, to the club army.
> What he meant to do? He asked what we had to do with that.
> Being required to lay down his arms, he said he would first lose
> his life; but was not so good as his word, for though he cocked
> and presented his musket, he was prevented, disarmed, and
> wounded, but not killed.

This countryman, who on his own defied the might of the New
Model Army, testified to the strength of feeling behind the rising
of the clubmen, but peasants howsoever heroic, and most were not
very heroic, could not defeat the force that had just conquered the
royalists at the battle of Naseby. His comrades on the hill fired on
Cromwell's men, but attacked by horsemen from front and rear,
they were overrun. Some cried 'Good Master Roundheads have

mercy upon me!', and others slid and tumbled down the steep slopes to escape. A number were killed and about 400 taken prisoner, of whom about half were wounded.

The clubmen wanted the local courts – the quarter sessions and the assizes – to function fully again. They upheld the ancient constitution of King, Lords and Commons, and believed that the issues of the Civil War should be resolved or laid to rest in a full and free parliament, consisting of the sovereign and all its members, both cavaliers and roundheads. They were against 'arbitrary government' and 'popery', and excluded 'papists' from their associations. They were against the radical religious sects and upheld the traditional Church of England as established by Queen Elizabeth. The sympathies of some of the clubmen inclined towards the royalists and of others towards the parliamentarians, but the ideology of the movement was neutrality. This was well expressed in *A Copy of a Petition* published at Exeter in 1645:

> Our intentions are to go on in a middle way; to preserve our persons and estates from violence, and plunder; to join with neither, and not to oppose either side, until by the answer to our petitions, we see who are the enemies of that happy peace, which we really desire. An accommodation in all reason is the happiest and speediest way to put an end to this bloody war, to root out popery, and all other sects contrary to the truth of God ...

If they were repelled from the king's cause it may have been because they were persuaded that he had subverted the old constitution by ruling without a parliament for eleven years from 1629 to 1640, and that he had betrayed the Protestant traditions of the Church of England: they associated him with 'arbitrary government' and 'popery'. If they were repelled from the parliament's cause it was probably because they linked it with the assumption of excessive power over the localities, with attacks on the traditional church, and with the radical religious sects. The risings of the clubmen exhibit four popular themes that ran through the English Revolution – support for the ancient constitution and the Elizabethan church, fear of 'papists' and dislike of 'sects'.

John Morrill describes the risings of the clubmen as 'the creation of the middling sort': 'they were led by, indeed initiated by, the middling sort ...' (Morrill 1976: 51; 1993: 210, 217). The risings did involve 'middling sort' but David Underdown sees them as 'revolts of whole communities', '... combining all levels of local society from lesser gentry to poor farmers in a move to defend the integrity of their communities against external threats' (Underdown 1980: 158; 1985: 157). There were gentry and clergy among the clubmen, but they seem to have joined after the risings began, probably with the aim of controlling the movement, and perhaps they were influential in putting the emphasis on petitioning for peace. The risings were in origins spontaneous movements of country people and were without authorisation from king or parliament or ruling class. They justified assembling in large numbers, arming themselves, and taking direct action against both the king's and the parliament's soldiers, by reference to the right of the people to defend themselves against oppression. Their efforts to organise a mass movement to end the Civil War, on their own initiative and independent of the constituted authorities, belong with the history of popular movements and of popular intervention in politics during the English Revolution.

There was concurrently popular discontent on another issue. At the heart of the revolt of the clubmen, on the borders of Wiltshire, Dorset and Somerset, lay the forest of Gillingham. The king's policy of disafforestation, extinction of common rights in the forest and enclosure of the land into separate farm holdings, had led to serious riots in Gillingham forest in 1626–28. Many poor cottagers with little land of their own had depended on the open forest for a large part of their livelihood, pasturing some animals there, poaching game, and taking wood for building and fuel. Many other poor cottagers worked in the cloth industry and had supplemented their wages with access to the resources of the open forest. When the forest was enclosed and granted by the king to the earl of Elgin, substantial farmers were well compensated for their loss of rights of common throughout the forest by grants of their own individual enclosed allotments, but the landless or near-landless cottagers got too little to make up for what they had lost. (Sharp 1980: 82–125, 159–60; 1985: 291–2; 1988: 124.)

With the outbreak of the Civil War, rioting was resumed in Gillingham forest and the enclosures were thrown down in 1642–43. The rioters defied both king and parliament, ignoring royal proclamations and telling the parliament men that they should have kept their orders and 'wiped their arses with them'. There was violence. The earl of Elgin was a parliamentarian but when his agent, Thomas Brunker, with his servants and the earl's tenants, tried to stop the riots, they were frequently assaulted, and they in turn shot and wounded some of the rioters, one of whom died in 1643 (Sharp 1980: 224–9, 232–3). The riots which began again at Gillingham forest in 1645 were associated with the risings of the clubmen. As the men of Gillingham and Motcombe gathered to go to the great meeting of the clubmen at Badbury Rings on 28 May they 'did tear up the hedges and made many gaps in the forest mounds'. On their return from the meeting the clubmen destroyed more enclosures. They beat off the servants of Brunker, who reported:

The club army which I feared would put boldness into them concerning our forest business, has brought them to this insolency, before they stood in some awe of commanders and soldiers, now they respect no man nor will give any obedience to any but contemn all superiors whatsoever and do what they please.

This throws additional light on the composition of the clubmen, for the rioters against the enclosures in Gillingham forest were mostly artisans, and the leader in 1643 was 'a poor linenweaver' and in 1645 a tanner (Sharp 1980: 240–2, 248). Their reasons for supporting the club movement were not the same as those of clergy, gentry and 'middling sort'.

This aspect of the rising of the clubmen may well explain in part why some of the gentry and clergy joined the movement: it may have been to control the poor cottagers, divert them from grievances against enclosures and keep them to campaigning for peace. The mass movement of the clubmen gave peasants and artisans the will and the courage to stand up for themselves against 'all superiors whatsoever' and to redress their grievances by direct action. It also throws more light on reasons for popular support for the clubmen and neutrality in the Civil War: the troubles of the poor cottagers of Gillingham forest were caused by the king and big landowners, but the 'middling sort' also benefited from the enclosures, which were defended by parliament. They had little reason to expect redress from either side in the Civil War. They were losers by the enclosures and losers by the Civil War, it was natural that opposition to both should fuse in their minds. They rose in arms to defend their livelihoods against both those who took the forest from them and those who would plunder their homes. Against enclosures they defended their customary rights and against the Civil War they defended the peace, the constitution, the laws, and the religion to which they had been accustomed.

Neutrals and clubmen were not able to stop the war: the New Model Army brought the war to an end by defeating royalists and neutrals.

CHAPTER 6

Revolution

... most of the oppressions of the commonwealth have in all times been brought upon the people by the king and lords ...

LEVELLER MANIFESTO, 1648

Seen from the high political level of parliament, the issues that had to be settled at the end of the Civil War concerned the power of the king – his control over his ministers, over the militia and over the church. The two Houses demanded that Charles's choice of ministers be subjected to approval by parliament. They sought to take control over the militia for 20 years, presuming that to be the remaining term of Charles's life (it was limiting the power of this particular monarch rather than of the monarchy that preoccupied the two Houses). The king resisted this, accepting the force of the advice that '... if you part with the militia and place [it] in the parliament as is desired you will thereby consent to change Monarchy into Aristocracy ...'. But the greatest obstacle to agreement between the two Houses and Charles was their demand that he consent to the abolition of episcopacy and its replacement by a Presbyterian form of church government. 'This alteration of government ... I believe to be as destructive to the regal power as the quitting of the militia', said the king. He regarded it as 'an infallible maxim' that 'the dependency of the church upon the crown is the chiefest support of regal authority'.

> It is not the change of church government which is chiefly aimed at ... but it is by that pretext to take away the dependency of the church from the crown, which ... I hold to be of equal consequence to that of the militia, for people are governed by pulpits more than the sword, in times of peace ... I will less yield to this than the militia ... . (Smith, David L. 1994: chs 5, 6.)

Seen from the lower political level, however, amongst those who supported and fought for parliament in the Civil War, questions arose whether the objective had been to preserve the old 'balanced' or 'mixed' constitution of King, Lords and Commons, with safeguards against Charles again abusing his power, or to establish the supremacy of the House of Commons, as the representative of the people, over both King and Lords? Had the objective been to replace the episcopalian state church by a Presbyterian state church, and was the latter to be like the former with everybody compelled to conform to it, or would it allow freedom to Protestant dissenters – Congregationalists, Baptists and other sects – to hold, practise and teach their different beliefs?

In July 1646 these questions were raised in London by *A Remonstrance of Many Thousand Citizens*, addressed to the House of Commons by the incipient Leveller movement:

> ... We do expect according to reason, that you should in the first place, declare and set forth King Charles's wickedness openly before the world, and withall, to show the intolerable inconveniences of having a kingly government, from the constant evil practices of those of this nation; and so to declare King Charles an enemy, and to publish your resolution, never to have any more, but to acquit us of so great a charge and trouble for ever ...

> You must also deal better with us concerning the Lords, than you have done. You only are chosen by us the people; and therefore in you only is the power of binding the whole nation, by making, altering, or abolishing of laws; you have therefore prejudiced us, in acting so, as if you could not make a law without both the royal assent of the king ... and the assent of the Lords ...

The assertion of the supremacy of the House of Commons was based on the belief that it derived its power from the people, and it was for the same reason that the petitioners insisted that parliament could not compel people in religion, because no such power had been delegated to it by the people.

> Whereas truly we are well assured, neither you, nor none else, can have any into power at all to conclude the people in matters that concern the worship of God, for therein every one of us ought to be fully assured in our own minds, and to be sure to worship him according to our consciences. You may propose what form you conceive best, and most available for information and well-being of the nation, and may persuade and invite thereunto, but compel you cannot justly; for you have no power from us so to do, nor could you have; for we could not confer a power that was not in ourselves, there being none of us, that can without wilful sin bind ourselves to worship God after any other way, than what (to a tittle) in our own particular understandings, we approve to be just. (Wolfe 1967: 113–30.)

Thus, as the people did not have the power to compel the consciences of each other, so they could not give that power to parliament. This drew the religious sects into radical politics because they sought constitutional guarantees for liberty of conscience.

Radical Londoners claimed a voice in the settlement of the nation, but what of the victorious New Model Army, which had the power to impose a settlement if it chose to use it? It is a matter of debate among historians how radical the soldiers were. At least half of the infantry were conscripts, who had been forcibly recruited from the lower ranks of society, mostly servants and labourers but including some small farmers and tradesmen. They served unwillingly, deserted when opportunity offered and were replaced by further resentful conscripts. Both sides filled their armies with conscripts and conscription was a long-standing popular grievance which the Levellers took up after the war. A contemporary said that most of the common soldiers in the infantry regiments of the New Model Army 'were ignorant men, of little religion ...', and a modern historian maintains that 'few of them had any political opinions ...'. But we cannot really know, and subsequent events seem to show that political and religious awareness among the foot soldiers can be underestimated. The men of the cavalry, however, were volunteers and generally of higher social class than the infantry. They included many London apprentices, who described themselves in a manifesto, *A Declaration of the Valiant Resolution of the Famous 'Prentices of London*, when they flocked to parliament's standard in 1642, as not being the 'mechanic scum of the people' or 'loose, idle fellows', but such as had 'trades and callings, and most of them young men of good parentage' whose families 'live honestly and thriftily in the country', and they made religion their 'object and cause'. By birth and vocation they belonged to the 'middle sort of people'. Cavalry was recruited by parliament from among yeomen, husbandmen, tradesmen and craftsmen, and their sons: ' ... cavalrymen like Thomas Ormes, the copyholder [tenant by the custom of the manor] of Felbrigg, and John Fitch, the Radwinter husbandman [small farmer], or Browne, the Cambridge tailor, Hurt the mason, Oliver the carpenter and Seman the son of a blacksmith of Bury St. Edmunds', may have been typical, writes Clive Holmes. Ian Gentles concludes that generally they were from 'the lower end of the scale of middling sort of people'. At the beginning of the war the officer corps had been dominated by substantial county gentry, but as the war went on it was diluted with minor gentry, and even plebeians won promotion to its ranks. (Holmes 1974: 164–8, 172–3, 175–7; Gentles 1992: 31–40.) There were many officers and soldiers who joined parliament's armies in order to fight for a cause and they were concerned how those issues would be settled for which they had taken up arms and risked their lives, and for which some of their comrades had died. There were religious and political radicals in the New Model Army – not necessarily the same persons – but they were a comparatively small minority and tended to be concentrated in certain regiments, especially of horse.

Nevertheless they were a leaven, and for numbers of men service in the New Model, in the infantry as well as the cavalry, was an education in radicalism.

Many soldiers were Londoners and some had links with the sectarian congregations in the capital, amongst which there was a growing agitation against the establishment of an intolerant Presbyterian state church. A radical political movement, soon to be nicknamed the Levellers, was emerging in London amongst small traders and craftsmen, many of them members of the sects. On 20 March 1647 it delivered a petition to the House of Commons, which it addressed as the 'supreme authority of this nation', asserting that a just government was one based on the supremacy of the representatives of the people, and demanding the abolition of the power of the king and the House of Lords to veto acts of the House of Commons. Further, it called for freedom from religious persecution:

> That all statutes, oaths and covenants may be repealed so far as they tend, or may be construed to the molestation and ensnaring of religious, peaceable, well-affected people, for non-conformity, or different opinion or practice in religion. That no man for preaching or publishing his opinion in religion in a peaceable way, may be punished or persecuted as heretical, by judges that are not infallible, but may be mistaken (as well as other men) in their judgements, lest upon pretence of suppressing errors, sects or schisms, the most necessary truths, and sincere professors thereof may be suppressed, as upon the like pretence it has been in all ages. (Wolfe 1967: 135–41.)

In a world in which the state church controlled education and most of the media of communication, freedom from its hegemony meant liberation from the cultural domination of the old hierarchical aristocratic order. The House of Commons rejected this petition and directed that it be burnt by the public hangman because it called in question the existing constitution of the state.

The Revolt of the New Model Army, 1647

Concurrently turmoil was precipitated in the army by the decision of parliament that only a small part of it would be retained as a standing force in England, and the rest would have to choose between engaging in the army to be raised for the reconquest of Ireland or being disbanded. At its start the agitation in the army was not inspired or organised by the Levellers: it arose independently and spontaneously amongst the rank-and-file soldiers (Kishlansky 1979: 180; Woolrych 1987: 64).

Towards the end of March 1647 a petition to parliament was circulating among the soldiers, but the officers persuaded the men to address it to the general of the army instead and to delete all matters that 'did not concern them properly as soldiers', that is, to leave out religious and political grievances and to confine themselves to objections to the terms offered by parliament for engagement for Ireland or disbandment. On those conditions many officers were prepared to support the petition, which demanded an act of indemnity for illegal actions committed by soldiers in performance of their military service, payment of a substantial part of the arrears in their wages and security for the rest, freedom in future from conscription for military service outside England for those who had joined the army voluntarily, and adequate provision for maimed soldiers and for the widows and children of those killed in the war. Parliament directed the general of the army, Sir Thomas Fairfax, to suppress this petition, which he tried to do, but it continued to circulate and gather signatures. On 30 March parliament declared that those who shall 'go on advancing and promoting that petition, shall be looked upon and proceeded against as enemies of the state and disturbers of the public peace'. This converted discontent into rebellion. The soldiers were infuriated by the denial of their right to petition (even their own general on matters concerning them as soldiers) and the slur on their honour to be branded 'enemies of the state and disturbers of the public peace' by the parliament for which they had just won victory in the Civil War. (Gardiner 1893: vol. III: 229, 248; Kishlansky 1979: 180–202; Woolrych 1987: 31–9; Gentles 1992: 149–52.) In protest, 151 officers signed a statement defending the banned petition and its demands, quoting parliament's own declaration of 2 November 1642 justifying the right of the people to petition: 'We hope, by being soldiers we have not lost the capacity of subjects, nor divested ourselves thereby of our interest in the commonwealth; that in purchasing the freedom of our brethren, we have not lost our own' (Woolrych 1987: 55–6).

Towards the end of April the private soldiers intervened decisively by organising themselves for protest and action. Each troop (in the case of a cavalry regiment) and each company (in the case of an infantry regiment) chose representatives to a regimental committee, which in turn selected two of its number to speak for the whole regiment: they were called 'agitators', which meant agents. This democratic organisation began in eight regiments of horse and in time spread to the foot and other regiments of horse. The representatives of the regiments formed a committee to promote the organisation of the rank-and-file throughout the army, to coordinate the actions of the regiments, and to direct resistance to parliament's terms for recruiting some regiments for Ireland and disbanding others (Gardiner 1893: vol. III: 247; Woolrych 1987: 61–3; Gentles 1992:

158–9, 175). The first appearance of elected representatives of the private soldiers caused considerable alarm in parliament, which sent the MPs who were also senior officers to quieten the distempers. They asked the officers to give accounts of the grievances of their regiments, but the officers replied that it would be unwise for them to do so without first consulting their men. It was agreed that each regiment would confer and submit a written report. This gave a further impetus to the organisation of the agitators, who played a major part in compiling the grievances of troops and companies and in drawing up the reports of the regiments. (Kishlansky 1979: 209–10; Woolrych 1987: 73.)

The regiments were under pressure from the senior officers to restrict their statements of grievances to matters which concerned them as soldiers – pay, indemnity, honour of the army – and most did, for obviously these would be the matters that worried them most immediately. But some regiments raised other matters which indicated anxiety about the fate of the cause for which they had been fighting. Colonel Harley's regiment of foot declared:

> That notwithstanding we have engaged our lives for you, ourselves, and posterity, that we might be free from the yoke of episcopal tyranny, yet we fear that the consciences of men shall be pressed beyond the light they have received from the rule of the Word in things appertaining to the worship of God ... (Firth and Davies 1940: vol. I: 360–4.)

Sir Hardress Waller's regiment of foot complained that 'we are denied the liberty which Christ has purchased for us ... to serve God according to our proportion of faith'. 'Faithful cordial godly men' were being discountenanced and ousted by 'ambidexters and neuters', and those who sought freedom to serve God according to the light of their consciences were 'like to be imprisoned, yea beaten and persecuted to enforce us to a human conformity never enjoined by Christ'. (Woolrych 1987: 82; Kishlansky 1979: 212.) Colonel Lambert's regiment of horse lamented the betrayal of the cause by the leaders of parliament:

> In the sadness of our spirit, we profess we can find little joy either disbanded or in arms, for whereas after so great expense of blood, treasure and time we look for the execution of justice but behold tyranny and oppression and that from those we had hoped under God had been the deliverers of our Israel, so that for anything as we conceive we can expect, none other but to be under as great slavery and bondage as we were before. (Kishlansky 1979: 215.)

General Fairfax's own regiment of horse did 'declare our averseness to the business of Ireland or disbanding till the real freedom of the free people of England be established'. And Commissary-General Ireton's regiment of horse gave as its chief grievance: 'That we are put upon the business of Ireland or else disbanding, before the real freedom of the people of England be established, according to the end wherefore this parliament was called, and the army raised for the preservation and defence of the same' (Woolrych 1987: 73–4). Only a minority of the soldiers may have felt this but it pointed to future developments in which the army would see itself as the embodiment of the cause for which the war had been fought, with the mission to settle the affairs of the nation to its satisfaction.

Instead of completing the ordinance to give the soldiers 'real and visible security' for their arrears of pay, the House of Commons decided on 25 May to proceed at once with the disbandment of the army. Over a period of two weeks the regiments were to be taken to separate rendezvous, in order to prevent concerted resistance across the army, and each soldier to be given the choice between service in Ireland or immediate cashierment with eight weeks of his arrears of pay. This was to start with Fairfax's own regiment of foot on 1 June at Chelmsford. The committee of agitators was being kept informed of decisions at Westminster by Lieutenant Edmund Chillenden, who wrote to them late at night on 25 May:

> Pray, gentlemen, ride night and day … If you do disappoint them in the disbanding of this regiment … you will break the neck of all their designs … Now, my lads, if we work like men we shall do well … You shall hear all I can, by the next, so till then I rest. Yours till death.

Three days later he reported that parliamentary commissioners and £7000 were being sent to Chelmsford to pay off Fairfax's regiment:

> Therefore, gentlemen, you know what to do … Therefore I pray be careful to have horse to apprehend and seize on the money and commissioners before they come at the foot. And if you can banish Jackson [lieutenant-colonel of the regiment] and the rest out of that regiment, you will do the work … So God bless, I rest, Yours … (Woodhouse 1938: 400–1.)

The decision of the committee of agitators to call upon the soldiers to refuse to obey the orders of parliament to disband was one of the most crucial of the revolution.

The agitators acted swiftly and vigorously to organise direct action by the rank-and-file to frustrate parliament's plans. They were now an independent power in the army, issuing orders which the soldiers obeyed. Parliament got word of the intention to seize the money for paying off Fairfax's regiment and recalled it just in time, and Fairfax sent three troops of horse to protect the parliamentary commissioners. But, acting under orders from the agitators, the men of Fairfax's regiment seized hold of the colours of their companies – at musket point in the case of an officer who resisted – and marched 1000-strong to a rendezvous near Braintree in Essex, on their way to join up with the main body of the army in order to prevent the regiments being picked off individually. The parliamentary commissioners sent Lieutenant-Colonel Jackson and Major Gooday after them, but as they approached the men cried out 'There come our enemies!', and when they produced copies of parliament's orders for disbanding 'they asked the officers, what do you bringing your tuppenny pamphlets to us?' They could do nothing with them, although some of the men said they would have been satisfied with four months' pay instead of the two months they were offered. The regiment marched off, effectively under the command of the only officer it would obey, the radical Captain Francis White who was working closely with the agitators. (Firth and Davies 1940: vol. I: 323–5; Woolrych 1987: 100–1, 105–6.)

Colonel Rainborough's regiment of foot was at Portsmouth awaiting embarkation for Jersey which was still in royalist hands. In his absence the regiment took instructions from the agitators, drove away its officers and set out to join Colonel Ingoldsby's regiment of foot at Oxford, in order to prevent parliament removing from there the train of artillery and its stores of ammunition. The House of Commons sent Rainborough to restore order in his regiment. He found it at Abingdon, and his account is interesting, coming from the most radical of the senior officers of the army.

> When I came, I found most of my officers come up to the general quarters of the regiment, who all that time till then had not dared so much as to appear amongst them. But they had not been long in their quarters, ere the major-serjeant was almost killed by his own soldiers; and his ensign, if he had not exceedingly well defended himself against another company, he had been cut all to pieces; but in defending himself he has wounded divers of them, two whereof, I am confident, cannot possibly escape with life. (Firth and Davies 1940: vol. II: 420.)

Colonel Ingoldsby's regiment was in garrison at Oxford and was due to be disbanded at Woodstock on 14 June. The sum of £3000 was dispatched from London to pay it off, but when parliament realised that the agitators knew of this, it tried to retrieve the money.

> The messenger being too slow, the money was got into Oxford before he could overtake it, and the soldiers, notwithstanding the parliament's commands, were resolved not to part with it. The convoy of dragoons who had guarded it from London attempted to have it back again, but the garrison soldiers fell

upon them in the High Street by All Souls College (where the money then stood) wounded several, and beat the rest so shamefully out of the city that they were glad not only to leave the money but a waggon and team of horses behind them. (Firth and Davies 1940: vol. I: 373–4.)

Under orders from the agitators, perhaps with the connivance of Cromwell, Cornet George Joyce of the General's lifeguard (a very radical unit) drew out a party of horse from several regiments, rode to Oxford to make sure the train of artillery and its ammunition was secure, and then to Holdenby House in Northamptonshire, where the king was a prisoner of the parliament, in order to prevent him being removed to London by Colonel Graves and parliament's commissioners. The troops guarding the king came over to Joyce and Colonel Graves fled. Austin Woolrych gives an account of Joyce's behaviour which illuminates the democratic movement in the army:

He told the king that he had his commission and his orders from 'the soldiery of the army', and in his own account he describes himself as 'an appointed agent by the army'. When his party arrived before Holdenby House and was asked who commanded it the men answered 'All commanded', and Joyce acted as their spokesman to the commissioners only 'by the unanimous consent of the party' ... Pressed by the commissioners to state his business in writing, he began thus: 'We, soldiers under his excellency Sir Thomas Fairfax's command, have, by the general consent of the soldiery ...'; indeed he acted throughout as *primus inter pares* in what can well be likened to a military soviet.

When Joyce and his party decided to take the king to the headquarters of the army and Charles asked him whose commission he had for what he was doing, Woolrych throws new light on his famous reply, pointing to the ranks of troopers behind him: 'Here is my commission':

Historians have taken this, as Charles did, for a confession that his only sanction was the sword, but Joyce surely meant just what he said: he derived his authority from the collective soldiery of the army, and exercised it by the advice and consent of those actually present. It is the most striking of many examples of the egalitarian camaraderie of the agitator movement, especially in its earlier phases. (Woolrych 1987: 106–15.)

Parts of the army were passing beyond Fairfax's control, and he called a meeting of all available officers on 29 May. 'I pray God the soldiers get not too much head', commented an observer at headquarters, 'the officers must instantly close with them, or else there will be disorder'. The great majority of the hundred officers who gathered at Fairfax's quarters was of the same opinion. They were presented with a petition signed by 31 agitators representing ten regiments of horse and six regiments of foot, calling for a general rendezvous of the whole army, accompanied by the clear threat they would order it themselves if Fairfax did not: 'we shall be enforced upon many inconveniences, which will of necessity arise when we (though unwillingly) shall be necessitated ... to do such things ourselves'. With 84 votes in favour, seven against and nine abstentions, the officers agreed to advise Fairfax to summon a general rendezvous of the army, giving as their reason that if he did not, it would take place without his authorisation. Fairfax told the Speaker of the House of Commons: 'I am forced to yield to something out of order, to keep the army from disorder, or worse inconveniences'. As Woolrych points out, the choice for Fairfax and his officers was 'between disobeying parliament or defying the organized will of their own men ...': they chose the former. Ian Gentles suggests that '... the great majority of officers opted to stay with their men, hoping that if they rode the back of the mutiny they would have a better chance of reining in its worst excesses' (Woolrych 1987: 100–4; Gentles 1992: 168). At the same time most of the officers probably sympathised with the resentment of their men against the way parliament had treated the army.

Little is known about most of the agitators beyond their bare names. William Allen, a trooper in Cromwell's regiment of horse and its representative, played a leading role in organising the rank-and-file of the eight regiments of horse in April, and emerged as a prominent spokesman for the agitators: he was a Baptist and in civilian life a feltmaker in Southwark. Several junior officers were involved with the agitators, notably Lieutenant Edmund Chillenden, a Baptist from Colonel Whalley's regiment of horse, who had been a button-seller in Cannon Street, London, and Cornet George Joyce who had been a tailor. Too much, however, should not be made of the influence of the radical religious sects because neither Joyce nor Edward Sexby, the prominent agitator from Fairfax's regiment of horse, are known to have been connected with sectarian congregations. (Tolmie 1977: 157–8, 160; Woolrych 1987: 84–6; Gentles 1992: 160.)

One vital factor that was to influence the actions of the army from now on was that its officers were no longer predominantly peers and greater gentry as they had been in the armies with which parliament began the Civil War. In the conflict between parliament and the New Model Army, about a quarter of the officers of the rank of captain-lieutenant and above supported parliament and either left or were driven out by their men. Eight colonels, two lieutenant-colonels, and seven majors were replaced by men who 'were on

the whole less socially distinguished and more politically militant
…'. Half of the officer corps now consisted of men who 'came from
backgrounds so obscure that no information can be recovered
about them':

> Of the remainder, nearly half came from the middle and lower
> ranks of society, especially from the towns. Only nine per cent
> of the total had received any higher education, and a sixth of
> them had definitely been promoted from the ranks. The highest
> levels of the corps contained more gentry, but also former
> artisans. (Gentles 1992: 168; Hutton 1990: 5.)

The rendezvous which changed the course of the English
Revolution took place near Newmarket on 4–5 June 1647. It was
attended by six regiments of horse and seven of foot. It adopted
the *Solemn Engagement of the Army*, by which it pledged not to be
divided or disbanded until its grievances were redressed, and it set
up a general council of the army, consisting of two officers and two
other ranks elected by each regiment, together with the generals,
which would formulate the demands of the army and decide when
they were satisfactorily met (Woodhouse 1938: 401–3). Thus the
existence of the agitators was formally recognised, they were incorporated into the power-structure of the army and they gained a voice
in its decision-making. But the senior officers saw the general
council as a device to re-establish a single chain of command in
the army, to eliminate the alternative centre of power based on the
rank-and-file, and to end the situation in which the agitators on
their own authority issued orders to the soldiers. The officers
generally looked to the restoration of discipline, putting an end to
the situation in which privates assaulted their officers and subalterns
defied their superiors. Increasingly the agitators themselves collaborated with the officers and the high command. Fairfax
maintained that the general council of the army did not replace his
own authority, in consultation with his council of war, in all military
matters, and that it existed only for the very specific purpose of
dealing with the present breach with parliament. He was given the
power of summoning and dissolving the general council, and later
he would use that power to get rid of it altogether. In order to be
politically effective, in order to outface parliament and its supporters
in London, and in order to deal with threats of a royalist revival,
the army needed unity, and it was easier for the soldiers to unite
under the authority of its established commander-in-chief, with his
record of military success, than under a variety of agitators who
were by no means all agreed in their opinions and strategies. At
the moment of their greatest triumph the power of the agitators
was already declining.

One fact, however, could not be changed, the New Model Army had become a political army, and neither officers nor men would be content to restrict their demands to pay and indemnity and their interests as soldiers rather than as citizens. An army cannot be immune from debates and disputes that divide the civilian population, especially one whose members were billeted upon the population and attended the same churches and frequented the same alehouses as civilians, and often had farms and trades and had enlisted for an emergency and not for a profession. Decisions had to be made about the future organisation of the state and the church, and the soldiers as Englishmen claimed the right to state their views on what they had fought for, and to speak for the people in whose cause they had risked their lives. On 14 June the army addressed parliament:

> Nor will it now, we hope, seem strange or unseasonable to rational and honest men ... if ... we shall, before disbanding, proceed in our own and the kingdom's behalf to propound and plead for some provision for our and the kingdom's satisfaction and future security ... Especially considering that we were not a mere mercenary army, hired to serve any arbitrary power of a state, but called forth and conjured by the several declarations of parliament to the defence of our own and the people's just rights and liberties. And so we took up arms in judgement and conscience to those ends, and have so continued ...

They would assert 'the just power and rights of this kingdom in parliament', by which they meant the supremacy of the people's representatives in the House of Commons, with the 'power of final judgements' in legislation, and the responsibility of those representatives to the people by being subject to regular elections for fixed terms. They denied that their intention was to prevent the setting up of the Presbyterian form of government in the church, but they desired that 'some effectual course' may be taken to provide liberty for 'tender consciences', and 'that such who upon conscientious grounds may differ from the established forms, may not for that be debarred from the common rights, liberties, or benefits belonging equally to all as men and members of the commonwealth, while they live soberly, honestly, inoffensively towards others, and peacefully and faithfully towards the state ...' (Woodhouse 1938: 403–9).

Counter-Revolution in London

London conceived of itself as being a sort of third estate of the realm: '... the magistracy of the city of London, the lord mayor, and court of common council being the greatest power next the king, and both Houses of Parliament, and having, next the king and the Houses, the greatest interest in the kingdom ...', declared a London manifesto. But after the Civil War there were two centres of power – the New Model Army and the city of London. State-power had collapsed: the king was a captive of the army and controlled no instruments of government, and the two Houses of Parliament, although in control of the machinery of government, were liable to be overawed by a London mob or by military force. The army turned itself into a united political power but London was divided in its politics and religion, and that weakened its ability to oppose the army as much as the fact that its military resources could not match those of the New Model.

Dominant elements in the parliament and the city were alarmed by the growth of the radical religious sects and by their supposed influence in the army, portending further extension of the revolution. A manifesto entitled *Some Queries propounded to the Common Council and Citizens of London* expressed in the summer of 1647 the fears of some parliamentarians and communicated them to the citizens:

> ... the work now on foot by chief agents in the army ... is not of yesterday, nor a business of not disbanding till full arrears, and an act of indemnity for the soldiery (however these have been held out as pretences, and made use of to draw the soldiery in, to carry on their designs long before laid) but 'tis a design and plot that has been laid these four years last past, by force of arms, an army of the sectarian modelling, to bring into this kingdom a general toleration of all religions, to destroy the civil government in the fundamental constitution of King, Lords and Commons, and to bring King Charles to justice (as they call it) as the grand delinquent in all the three kingdoms ... ; to possess themselves of, and be masters of the city of London; to get to themselves and their party all the estates, riches, and great places of the kingdom, and to rule all by an arbitrary new modelled government of their own setting up, and by a perpetual army ...

A powerful movement had developed, led by influential London clergy and members of the city government, demanding the disbandment of the army and the suppression of the sects. It sought to prevent revolutionary excesses and to consolidate the revolution by replacing episcopacy with Presbyterianism. Under the latter the church would not be governed by bishops appointed by the king but by assemblies of the clergy and representatives of the laity, and the parish elites would be associated as lay elders with the ministers in imposing a 'godly discipline' on the parishes, especially on the poor. In order to make a settlement they had to come to terms with Charles I, but he would not accept Presbyterianism, except perhaps

as a short-term expedient to regain his power but not in the long-term. On the other hand, the army would not accept a Presbyterian church unless it allowed liberty for 'tender consciences' to separate from it, but a Presbyterian settlement was wanted by its supporters precisely to prevent that liberty. Thus there was deadlock.

In this situation, unrest among the populace of London ran parallel to unrest among the private soldiers of the army, and both influenced the events of 1647 crucially. Two incidents illustrate first of all the potential for turmoil in London.

The taxes which parliament had imposed to fight the war were far heavier than any experienced before and extended much further down the social scale. Now that the fighting had stopped these taxes were resented more than ever, but they could only be reduced if the army were disbanded. One of these taxes was the excise which, as a sales tax on items of common consumption such as beer, salt and meat, fell more heavily on the poor than on the rich. On 15 February 1647 there was a riot against the excise at Smithfield market in London: the collectors were beaten up, their books destroyed, £80–100 taken from them, and their office burnt down. The lord mayor and sheriffs had to come in person to restore order. (Gardiner 1893: vol. III: 216; Pearl 1972: 38–40, 43; Braddick 1991: 597.)

The second incident involved disregard of the godly discipline which the Presbyterians were so anxious to enforce. It took place on Moorfields, north of London, where citizens were accustomed to go for recreation on Sundays. On Sunday 21 March 1647 the constable and officers of Shoreditch parish made a sweep through the victualling places and alehouses, which crowded around Moorfields, in order to enforce parliament's ordinance for the observation of the sabbath, and to stop people drinking when they should have been at church hearing the sermon. They discovered apprentices tippling in the Ship alehouse but their attempt to arrest them provoked a riot. They managed to drag three apprentices to the house of a JP, Thomas Hubbert, followed by a large crowd which smashed the windows, and when fired on, broke in and ransacked the house. The trained bands were called out to restore order.

Most accounts described the rioters as apprentices but Hubbert in his own report, *A Brief and True Relation of the great disorders and riot attempted and committed upon the house and goods of Thomas Hubbert, Esquire*, insisted that 'the city apprentices had the least hand in this high offence, only some few that were provoked and set on by the multitude …'. The chief offenders, he said, 'were idle, loose, and profane livers, masterless men, and such as have been out in the wars, and housekeepers [i.e. householders] that have spent and consumed their fortunes in sinful and irreligious courses …'. Hubbert may have been somewhat disingenuously adopting stereotypical views of the types of persons assumed to commit disorders, but he identified precisely those whom the Presbyterian godly discipline was intended to control. There was evidently more behind this riot than the victimising of three apprentices, for the crowd took Hubbert's papers and tore up his leases, indicating that he was probably an unpopular landlord. According to *Strange and Terrible News from Moorfields*, the mob stole plate and money to the value of £300–400 and 'one of the justice's best cloaks', implying in the light of Hubbert's own account hostility of the poor towards the rich.

The apprentices were one of the best organised groups in London, with a proven capacity for collective action. In 1647 they had an agenda of their own. The abolition by parliament of the numerous traditional religious holidays as superstitious relics of popery, and the strict rules of Sunday observance, left the apprentices without days for recreation. They organised a campaign of petitions and demonstrations, involving also servants and schoolboys, for one day's holiday each month, or 'play-day' as the press dubbed it. They persuaded a reluctant parliament to make the second Tuesday in each month a holiday for 'all scholars, apprentices, and other servants', but subject to 'the leave and approbation of their masters respectively first had and obtained'. This did not satisfy the apprentices and the threat of further mass demonstrations persuaded parliament to amend the ordinance to the effect that masters should normally grant the holiday except in cases of 'urgent necessity' in their businesses or trades. When the first holiday took place on Tuesday 13 July, however, some masters would not shut their shops and sacked their servants who took the day off. (Gardiner 1893: vol. III: 324–5; Smith, Steven R. 1978–79: 318; Braddick 1991: 615.) So on the eve of the involvement of apprentices in national politics in 1647, their relations with their masters were strained, and as one of their petitions pointed out '... there is a great difference wrought both in the affections and inclinations, betwixt master and servant ...', and spoke of '... the hard usage and slavish bondage borne and endured by many apprentices and servants in this city and kingdom ...'. It is unlikely, therefore, that in the ensuing events the apprentices were acting merely at the behest of the masters.

Politically the apprentices were divided. In the quarrel between the parliament and the army, some supported the former and others the latter. Both groups of apprentices took advantage of their newly won holiday on 13 July to engage in political activity. One group demanded that the army be disbanded 'so this almost exhausted kingdom may be freed from those many grievous taxes and oppressions it now groans under'; that the government of the church be speedily settled, toleration not allowed and the sects suppressed; and that the king be restored to 'his just power'. Like the soldiers they drafted a *Solemn Engagment* and chose agitators in the wards of the city to canvass for signatures, and also to mobilise the support of seamen and watermen (the latter rowed passengers along and across the river Thames, London's main highway). The key to the control of the city lay in the hands of the London trained bands. Parliament returned control of the bands to the city government, which proceeded to purge radicals from commands. The dominant faction in parliament and the city government hoped to be able to deploy the bands as a counter-force to the army. The other group of apprentices protested against this in concert with the agitators of the army, who congratulated them rather patronisingly on being 'so public spirited as to have the good of the people in your eyes rather than such things as ... days of recreation and the like, though not unfitting in themselves ...'. Under pressure from the army, parliament took back control of the trained bands and restored radicals to their commands. At this the rival group of apprentices broke out in fury and, supported by ex-soldiers, seamen and watermen, blockaded and occupied parliament on 26 July, forcing the members to vote at their dictation to return the trained bands again to the control of the city, and to bring the king to London to treat without any preconditions. Amongst the leaders of the mob were some of the apprentices who had been organisers of the campaign for a monthly holiday. Bulstrode Whitelocke, a Member of Parliament, exclaimed: 'Here ... you may observe an instance of the highest insolence in the rabble and of popular madness that you can meet with in any other story.'

The apprentices were a select group and hoped when they had served their time to set up their own businesses and to have the potential to rise to high places in the companies and government of London. Thus they had an interest both in the state of the city's economy and in the privileges and powers of its companies and government. When they called for the trained bands to be returned to the control of the city their petition spoke of maintaining and defending 'the franchises and liberties of this honourable city, to which we are the apparent heirs'. Thus the apprentices were moved by concern to uphold the independence of London's government by having it control the city's trained bands, and to free the king from pressure to come to terms with the army and to have him come to terms in effect with London.

The actions of the apprentices pushed London towards a showdown with the army, but they also produced a backlash. Opponents of the army in parliament and the city government could not hope to succeed without popular support, and they seized upon the shift of power engineered by the apprentices to begin to organise armed resistance in London to the army. But the events of late July made clear to the middle ranks of citizens – the masters of shops and workshops – and to the wealthier citizens the dangers of popular disorder, the difficulties of parliament and city government in controlling mobs, and the risk of surrendering direction to a popular movement whose agenda might exceed or differ from their own. Sir Lewis Dyve, a royalist prisoner in the Tower of London, reported to the king: '... the city in a manner reduced into an absolute anarchy, the 'prentices, watermen and seamen governing all in effect by their agitators, according to the example given them by the army, slighting all orders issued, both from the Houses and the magistracy of the city ...'. Eight peers and 58 MPs with the Speakers of both Houses, fled from the violence of the mob to the shelter of the army, which marched on London to restore a 'free parliament'. Resistance to the army collapsed, because it was opposed by influential clergy and by many inhabitants, especially in Southwark and the suburbs; because it seemed impossible that the city's forces could withstand the army; and because armed conflict would risk great damage to the trade and property of the citizens. Underlying this was acceptance that control by a disciplined army was preferable to control by an undisciplined mob. (Gardiner 1893: vol. III: 335–9; Pearl 1972: 33, 49–52, 54–6; Smith, Steven R. 1978–79: 319–22; Kishlansky 1979: 258–9, 264–70; Adamson 1987: 567–9; Braddick 1991: 616–17; Brenner 1993: 479–80). However, the question of the settlement of religious and political issues was still unresolved.

The 'Agreement of the People'

When the elected representatives of the officers and of the other ranks came to consider in the general council of the army the details of a 'happy settlement' of the kingdom, they were faced with two schemes: first of all with one drafted by Commissary-General Ireton and Colonel Lambert, in concert with some members of the Lords and Commons, known as the *Heads of Proposals*, and then with one composed by some agitators in concert with the London Levellers, entitled the *Agreement of the People*. The difference between these lay in fundamentally opposed concepts. The concept underlying the *Heads* was one which so far had dominated the parliamentarian party: that there was an ancient constitution of King, Lords and Commons, which had existed from time immemorial, governed by fundamental laws from which were derived the prerogatives of kings, the privileges of parliaments' and the rights of subjects. But from time to time kings abused their prerogatives, parliaments exceeded their privileges, and subjects mistook their rights, and such had to be corrected. The *Heads* retained the structure of King, Lords and Commons, and the veto (or 'negative voice' as it was termed at the time) of the king and the Lords over

proposals of the Commons. They did not seek to change the constitution but to reform it, by making effective the power of parliament
to limit the king and by ensuring the responsibility of parliament
to the people. In contradistinction, the Levellers held that the
ancient constitution had been imposed by force on the people
after the Norman conquest in 1066, from which the present king
ultimately derived his title and his prerogatives, but that conquest
was now reversed by the victory of the people over Charles I in the
Civil War. Power now reverted to its only rightful source, the
people, who must make anew the constitution by *Agreement of the
People*. That would embody the fundamental principle that just power
was derived from the consent of the people, which meant the
ending of the veto of the king and the Lords, since they did not
represent the people, and subordinating them to the Commons
which did, or should, represent the people. But the Commons would
be supreme only in the matters delegated to it by the people, and
the distinctive feature of this new constitution was that it would
lay down what the Commons could and could not do. Therefore
the *Agreement* bridled not only the king and the Lords but also the
Commons in the interest of the sovereignty of the people (Woolrych
1987: 221–2). Thus the Levellers rejected the traditional idea of
the constitution as a form of 'mixed government' – King, Lords
and Commons, or monarchy, aristocracy and democracy – that was
held by parliament and the *Heads of Proposals*.

A rift opened up between the reformist tendency of the *Heads
of Proposals* and the revolutionary tendency of the *Agreement of the
People*. This was the subject of the famous debates in the general
council of the army at Putney in October–November 1647, and
Cromwell recognised the issue in his immediate response to first
hearing the *Agreement* read: 'Truly this paper does contain in it very
great alterations of the very government of the kingdom, alterations
from that government that it has been under, I believe I may
almost say, since it was a nation ...' (Woodhouse 1938: 7). The
survival of a fairly full record of speeches on the question of the
franchise in parliamentary elections has led historians to focus on
this at the expense of other issues that may have been more crucial
but for which a less full record of speeches survives. It was the future
of the monarchy and the House of Lords which was now becoming
the central issue of the revolution, and questions were being asked,
not about the terms on which Charles I should be restored to
power, but whether he should be made accountable for causing the
Civil War.

Maximilian Petty, a civilian, speaking for the Levellers in the
debates, said:

I had the happiness sometimes to be at the debate of the *Proposals*, and my opinion was then as it is now, against the king's vote and the Lords'. But I did not then so definitely desire the abolition of these votes as I do now desire it; for since that time it has pleased God to raise a company of men [i.e. the Levellers] that do stand up for the power of the House of Commons, which is the representative of the people, and deny the negative voice of king and Lords ... For my part I cannot but think that both the power of king and Lords was ever a branch of tyranny. And if ever a people shall free themselves from tyranny, certainly it is after seven years' war and fighting for their liberty. For my part I think that if the constitution of this kingdom shall be established as formerly, it might rivet tyranny into this kingdom more strongly than before.

Captain Francis Allen (an officer-agitator from Colonel Ingoldsby's regiment of foot), fresh from a prayer-meeting, declared that God had answered the prayers of himself and 'divers other godly people: that the work that was before them was to take away the negative voice of the king and Lords' (Woodhouse 1938: 89, 95–6).

Captain John Carter confessed 'that he found not any inclination in his heart (as formerly) to pray for the king ...'; and Lieutenant-Colonel William Goffe said that the generals had sinned in negotiating with the king over the *Heads of Proposals*: 'And it has so wrought with me that ... I dare not open my mouth for the benefit or upholding of that kingly power: I think that has been the voice of God ...'. Lieutenant-Colonel John Jubbes, a London radical in Colonel Hewson's regiment of foot, raised the question whether the king was 'guilty of all the bloodshed, vast expense of treasure, and ruin that has been occasioned by all the wars ...'. Captain George Bishop interjected:

I shall desire to speak one word ... After many enquiries in my spirit what's the reason that we are distracted in counsel, and that we cannot, as formerly, preserve the kingdom from that dying condition in which it is, I find this answer, the answer which is vouchsafed to many Christians besides, amongst us ... I say that the reason is a compliance to preserve that man of blood, and those principles of tyranny, which God from heaven by his many successes given has manifestly declared against, and which, I am confident, may yet be our destruction if they be preserved.

Trooper Edward Sexby, agitator of Fairfax's regiment of horse, declared:

We have gone about to wash a blackamoor, to wash him white, which he will not. We are going about to set up that power which

God will destroy; I think we are going about to set up the power of kings, some part of it, which God will destroy, and which will be but a burdensome stone that whosoever shall fall upon it, it will destroy him. (Woodhouse 1938: 96, 99–101, 103, 107.)

The scene is thus set for the climax of the revolution in 1648–49. The Levellers had emerged and changed the terms of the debate; the army had entered politics and altered the balance of power. In order to become a fully revolutionary force the army needed an ideology, the Levellers now offered it. Although much was to happen between the autumn of 1647 and the autumn of 1648, including a renewal of Civil War precipitated by the king, from which the New Model Army again emerged victorious; and although there was no inevitability about the outcome, it was prepared by the revolt of the army in 1647.

The Military *Coup d'état* of 1648–1649

On 11 September 1648 a petition was presented to the House of Commons with, it was claimed, 40,000 signatures. It was organised by the Levellers and came to be regarded by them as the basic programme of their party. Its primary function was to condemn parliament for continuing to negotiate with Charles I and the terms on which they were preparing to restore him to power.

> ... Yet considering upon what grounds we engaged on your part in the late and present wars, and how far (by our so doing) we apprehend ourselves concerned, give us leave (before you conclude us by the treaty in hand) to acquaint you first with the ground and reason which induced us to aid you against the king and his adherents ... Be pleased therefore to understand, that we had not engaged on your part, but that we judged this honourable House to be the supreme authority of England, as chosen by, and representing the people, and entrusted with absolute power for redress of grievances, and provision for safety; and that the king was but at the most the chief public officer of this kingdom, and accountable to this House (the representative of the people, from whom all just authority is, or ought to be derived) for discharge of his office ...

It criticised parliament for declaring that it would not alter the ancient government from that of King, Lords and Commons, without considering, in case of differences between them, which should have the final say.

> And when as most of the oppressions of the commonwealth have in all times been brought upon the people by the king and Lords, who nevertheless would be so equal in the supreme

authority, as that there should be no redress of grievances, no provision for safety, but at their pleasure. For our parts, we profess ourselves so far from judging this to be consistent with freedom or safety, that we know no great cause wherefore we assisted you in the late wars, but in hope to be delivered by you from so intolerable, so destructive a bondage ...

They said that they had long expected:

That you would have made good the supreme authority of the people, in this honourable House, from all pretences of negative voices, either in king or Lords.

That you would have made laws for election of representatives yearly and of course without writ or summons.

That you would have set express times for their meeting, continuance and dissolution ... and to have fixed an expressed time for the ending of this present parliament.

That you would have done justice upon the capital authors and promoters of the former or late wars ...

That you would have laid to heart all the abundance of innocent blood that has been spilt, and the infinite spoil and havoc that has been made of peaceable harmless people, by express commissions from the king; and seriously to have considered whether the justice of God be likely to be satisfied, or his yet continuing wrath appeased, by an act of oblivion.

The petitioners returned to the House on 13 September and 'became so bold as to clamour at the very door against such members as they conceived cross to their designs; and said they resolved to have their large petition taken into consideration before a treaty [with the king]; that they knew no use of a king or Lords any longer; and that such distinctions were the devices of men, God having made all alike'. H.N. Brailsford comments that this petition and demonstration '... cut a channel for the main current of revolutionary opinion in the country, and swept the army into action'. (Wolfe 1967: 279–90; Tolmie 1977: 176–7; Brailsford 1961: 349–57).

It was believed that England had been defiled by the blood shed in the civil wars, and that the Bible provided ample evidence that God would punish the nation for this unless it executed justice upon the person or persons accountable. If it failed to do this the whole people would share in the sin and be scourged by God. The soldiers especially, at whose hands the blood had been shed, needed to be absolved from the guilt and redeemed from God's punishment, by fixing responsibility and executing justice. They concluded that responsibility lay with the king, 'the capital and grand author of all our troubles', and resolved to bring him 'to an account for the

blood he has shed' (Hill 1993: 96–8, 324–9). At the same time millenarian beliefs, which had spread in parliament's party and army,
prophesied the imminence of the Second Coming of Jesus Christ
to establish his kingdom on earth and rule it through his 'saints'
('the godly'). The rule of King Charles would be replaced by that
of King Jesus. Very diverse views of a future society were projected
onto the millennium, but they had this in common that they
visualised a very different society from that which existed at the
present. It was not just blood-guilt which drove forward the
revolution at this stage but intense hope and real expectation of
radical change. Thomas Collier preached to the army on the text
from Isiah 'Behold I create new heavens and a new earth'. The earth,
he said, would no longer be governed by wicked men but Christ
'will in and by his saints rule the world'. In the hands of radicals
this was not a passive doctrine of waiting patiently for the Second
Coming, but an obligation upon 'the godly' to 'help forwards this
great work and design of God'. They must prepare the way for the
millennium by securing liberty of conscience so that they would
no longer 'be subject to men in the things of God' but only to God.
They must deliver the people from the burden of tithes (compulsory
levies for the support of the clergy), from 'tyrannical and oppressing
laws and courts', and from 'whatsoever bears but the face of
oppression'. Collier maintained that there was an obligation on the
army to promote this, because 'the people in their petitions call for
it daily', '… and certainly God calls for it at your hands' (Woodhouse
1938: 390–6; Capp 1972: chs 2, 3).

The Leveller petition of 11 September 1648 was followed by
petitions from radical groups in numerous counties and towns
calling for breaking off negotiations with the king and bringing him
to justice. For example, the mayor, aldermen and common council
of Newcastle upon Tyne warned parliament: '… for if we would
never bow the knee to Baal at the king's command, we will never
bow it at the parliament's, and if they act against the trust reposed
in them by the people, the people are bound in conscience and duty
to act against them, *salus populi* being *suprema lex*'. They condemned
parliament men for being willing to sell their freedom and birthrights
for 'a mess of pottage, so that they may enjoy a slavish peace'. A
flood of petitions from the regiments and garrisons of the army
demanded that the king be put on trial, and more than half of them
expressed support for the Leveller petition of 11 September.
(Howell 1967: 203–4; Underdown 1971: 108–10, 115–21; Gentles
1992: 268.) At the beginning of December the army occupied
London and excluded from their seats in parliament those members
who sought to continue negotiations with the king (known as
'Pride's Purge' after the colonel who executed it).

The officers saw a need to work with the minority of MPs who survived the purge and continued to sit at Westminster, and with the groups of religious and political radicals in London and the provinces, especially with the Levellers. It was not their intention to establish military rule or a military dictatorship and they debated with the Levellers the shape of a constitutional settlement. '... The Levellers were an important factor in the calculations of the army leadership and their ideas were treated seriously at the time of the revolution in late 1648 and early 1649 ...', writes Derek Massarella. 'By the closing weeks of 1648, though the king's removal was all but certain, only the Levellers had developed a comprehensive plan for alternative government', says Barbara Taft. (Massarella 1981: 46–7; Taft 1985: 70–1; Gentles 1992: 289, 292.) The Levellers held the intellectual initiative from 11 September onwards. In consultation with representatives of the officers and of London sectaries they produced a new version of the *Agreement of the People*, which the council of officers – there were no representatives of the other ranks on the council since 1647 – began to debate on 11 December. A rift developed between the Levellers and the officers. The officers insisted on amending the *Agreement* and submitting it to the purged parliament for approval, but this destroyed the whole point of the *Agreement*, which was that it should derive from the consent of the people and be a law superior to parliament, unalterable by parliament and determining what parliament could and could not do. It should therefore, in the Levellers' view, be submitted directly to the people unamended. The Levellers walked out of the discussions with the council of officers, which nevertheless continued for five weeks to study and debate the *Agreement*, and adopted many of the ideas and much of the programme of the Levellers.

These discussions involved 124 officers, who were advised by 30 clergy. Barbara Taft finds that the leading part was played by a core of 21 officers ranging from generals to captains. Of these, one came from the greater gentry, four (possibly five) from the lesser gentry, two had professional backgrounds, and six 'were from merchant families or were themselves small tradesmen'. The latter ranged 'from Richard Deane, whose great uncle had been lord mayor of London, through Thomas Harrison, son of a prosperous butcher, and Robert Tichborne, a linen-draper, to John Okey, a ship chandler'. Colonel John Hewson, usually described as 'of mean parentage and brought up to the trade of a shoemaker', may have been a cadet of a landed family in Kent and he was a substantial shoemaker, and George Joyce, promoted to captain since his exploit in arresting the king at Holdenby in 1647, was a tailor, though whether poor or prosperous cannot be ascertained. The origins of the remaining seven are obscure 'but their careers suggest that they came from families of the middling sort' (Taft 1985: 173–5). Taft and Gentles conclude that the proposals for a constitutional settlement which emerged from the council of officers represented a victory for the junior officers over their superiors: Commissary-General Ireton (Cromwell's son-in-law), the most effective but voluble spokesman for the senior officers, was defeated in five out of the seven recorded divisions. (Taft 1985: 175–7; Gentles 1992: 291.)

The officers drove forward the trial of the king and his execution on 30 January 1649, the abolition of the monarchy and the House of Lords, and the establishment of a republic.

The impetus for the revolutionary *coup d'état* of December 1648 to January 1649 came not only from the officers and soldiers but also from political and religious radicals in London and the provinces. In Somerset the petition in support of the trial of Charles I was drafted by the Baptist minister Thomas Collier, and promoted by a radical squire, a yeoman and a clothier. The Kent petition for justice on the king found considerable support in the traditional radical centres of the Weald, which was a region with iron and cloth industries, few gentry and many poor people, with a history of radicalism stretching from the Lollards in the fifteenth century to 'a host of sectaries' and 'a strong Leveller movement' at the present. Notable support for the coup came from Newport Pagnell in Buckinghamshire and this was another place which had long been a centre of religious dissent and 'a hotbed of radical discussion'. In London the lead in backing the coup was taken by some radical clergy and by some of the merchants engaged in colonial trades and plantations, the 'new merchants' described in Chapter 4.

'Divers well-affected inhabitants of the cities of London and Westminster, borough of Southwark, Tower Hamlets, and parts adjacent', declared in December their intention of joining with the army 'in their just proceedings against all unjust persons whatsoever, who have betrayed the trust reposed in them …'. 'Many thousand public spirited persons' in Portsmouth, Southampton, the Isle of Wight, Poole, Weymouth and Malmesbury united with the officers and soldiers of the garrisons in those places 'for the redemption of our native rights and freedoms'. 'Many thousands' of the 'well-affected' at Halifax, Leeds, Bradford, Preston and Mansfield declared their support for government without a king or House of Lords, and offered to assist the northern brigade of the army against any opposition. These were voices from the northern cloth-making districts. In the southwest there seems to have erupted a not inconsiderable popular movement in support of the coup. A radical wrote from Tavistock on 10 November 1648:

The Lord we see is now breaking forth his terrible judgements upon all the enemies of his people; he has bound their kings with chains, and their nobles with fetters of iron, and he will not spare any that seek [his people's] ruin, no, his glory is breaking out to disperse all foggy vapours and designs against them, and will nakedly lay open all their wickedness, to their shame and confusion. We are all fixed, and ready, with many thousand well-affected in these parts, to act what God shall put us upon, for his glory and the people's freedom, which he will never suffer to be taken from them by any pretended authority, or arbitrary power whatsoever.

'The Lord has raised up the spirits of all the honest party in this county, and near us', another radical wrote on 24 December from Somerton in Somerset, 'in relation to the late proceedings of the parliament and army, for common justice, freedom, and preservation, that we are no less than 12,000 horse and foot listed to join with and engage for the ends mentioned ...'. 'Many hundreds' of the 'well-affected' in Plymouth, Tavistock and other places in the southwest resolved to live and die with the army and the purged parliament, and a large crowd of the 'well-affected' met at Taunton and declared their resolution 'to sacrifice lives and fortunes in the defence of parliament and army, for the obtaining of justice, liberty, and freedom, together with the common rights of the people of England'. No doubt there was much exaggeration and wishful thinking by the radicals, but John Turberville (a London lawyer who lived at Tolland near Wiveliscombe in Somerset) thought that the country was on the verge of a Leveller revolution and expected 'men and horses to be raised and the *Agreement of the People* to be sent into every parish for subscriptions'. (Manning 1992: 24–7, 34–6; Brenner 1993: 533–47.)

The *Agreement of the People* was not implemented. Although the officers presented their version of it to the House of Commons on 20 January 1649, they acquiesced when it was ignored. The underlying difference between the Levellers and the officers, politicians and clergy who seized direction of the revolution, was that in deriving power from the people, the former meant the subordination of parliament to the people who elected it, but the latter meant the subordination of the people to their representatives in parliament (in reality such representatives as had not been purged by the army). Thus the revolution was carried through by a purged parliament rather than by the election of a new parliament or constituent assembly. By the *Agreement* parliament would have dissolved before the end of April 1649 and a new one been elected on a reformed franchise and with a redistribution of seats, but the purged parliament (or 'Rump Parliament' as it would later be

nicknamed) continued in power until 1653. Many of the revolutionaries feared that free elections on a broad franchise, as desired
by the Levellers, would have brought opponents of the revolution
to power. The Levellers lost much of their strength when many of
the sectaries, from whom a great deal of their support had come,
were bought off with a large measure of religious toleration and
dropped the Levellers' constitutional programme, though not their
proposals for reform of the legal system and of tithes.

Displacement of the Ruling Class from Political Power

'The plain fact is that by 1646–48', writes G.E. Aylmer, 'a majority
of the peerage, of the upper gentry, and of the prewar urban elites
were either forcibly excluded from government, or had withdrawn
into alienated isolation from it; while from 1649 on this is true of
the overwhelming majority of peers, baronets, knights, and prewar
esquires, or their respective sons and heirs' (Aylmer 1980: 151–2).
Ronald Hutton says that in the 1650s '... no more than a fraction
of the nobility and greater gentry of England and Wales were still
either allowed or prepared to serve the regime, so that the economic
and social rulers of the country mostly remained outside the power
structure' (Hutton 1990: 79–80). The ruling class was displaced
from political power during the revolution, though this took place
gradually and unevenly and was never total, but they were not
deprived of their wealth or status, which meant that their exclusion
from political power was unlikely to be permanent.

In order to fight the Civil War parliament had created new
organs of government in the provinces – committees which took
over the running of the counties. Some of these committees were
dominated by that fraction of the ruling class which supported
parliament, others were composed to a significant extent of men
below the level of the ruling class. In Warwickshire the committee
was controlled by minor gentry and Coventry merchants (Hughes
1987: 169, 174–80). As the war went on this became more common.
In Lincolnshire from 1644 the government of the county devolved
upon men of 'lesser rank' than its previous rulers (Holmes 1980:
187). In Somerset power moved from 'solid county families' to men
'who before the war could never have aspired to the upper reaches
of county government' – lesser gentry, townsmen, yeomen's sons,
and 'others on or outside the fringes of gentility' (Underdown
1973: 47, 124–5, 152; 1985: 225). After the victory of parliament
in the Civil War changes took place in more counties. In Kent greater
gentry lost control of county government to army officers, local
lawyers, but chiefly lesser gentry. (Everitt 1966: 143–4, 151–2,
154–5, 296–7, 329; Clark 1977: 392–3.) 'There was a remarkable

shift in the territorial basis of power' in Glamorgan, where 'the power of the great landowners was temporarily broken' and a 'group of radical small squires' took over (Roberts 1986: 226, 232–4, 245–7).

The process of displacing the old ruling class was carried further by the *coup d'état* of 1648–49, although in some counties, for example Suffolk, Sussex and Devon, a section of the prewar governors clung to a large part of power, albeit having to accept a bigger role for minor gentry. (Everitt 1960: 36; Fletcher 1975: 57, 132–4, 300–1, 316; Roberts 1985: 27–8, 148, 157.) After the king's execution greater gentry lost their majority on the Lancashire committee to minor gentry and plebeians, who were generally less wealthy than their predecessors (Blackwood 1978: 80–4). In 1649 the Herefordshire committee continued to have 'representatives of the traditional county elite', but there was a significant increase of 'middling and lesser gentry' and of 'professional men (lawyers, physicians and so on) or men with commercial rather than landed interests, usually called gentlemen' but not recognised as such before the war (Aylmer 1972: 381–2). 'In Lincolnshire half of the men who had been involved in the administration of the county prior to the army's coup were dismissed from office. Their places ... were taken almost exclusively by parvenus – minor gentry for the most part', but also lawyers and men recently risen from yeoman status: it was these new men, rather than the few surviving members of the old county elite, who became 'the backbone of local administration' (Holmes 1980: 207).

During the 1650s county government reverted back to the JPs and changes in the magisterial bench became significant. In Cheshire there were 30 men who were active JPs between 1645 and 1659 'but only nine of these belonged to families represented on the bench between 1603 and 1642 ...'. The places of the prewar governing elite were taken by middling gentry mostly, but also by some minor gentry on the borderline with the yeomanry (Morrill 1974: 184, 186–7, 223–5, 233–4, 256–8). Between 1645 and 1660 only four of the 42 men named as JPs for Warwickshire had been on the bench before the war, although the fathers of four more had been. Before 1642 all JPs were leading county gentry, but six of the interregnum justices were not even of gentry origins, 'and the actual government of the county was undertaken mainly by comparatively minor gentry' (Hughes 1987: 272). In Lancashire '... the greater gentry had a monopoly of the bench before 1642, a near-monopoly in the late 1640s and a bare majority in the 1650s. Those who gained most from the social changes of the interregnum were the lesser gentry', but there were also four plebeians, and '... during the interregnum there was a marked fall in the proportion of rich and middle-income magistrates' (Blackwood 1978: 77–80).

After 1649 the local militias were reorganised to defend the revolution rather than to bolster the power of the ruling class. In Somerset the militia officers were now 'far less substantial than would have been conceivable in earlier days' and indeed included as captains not only minor gentry but also men of lower status: 'William Venicombe was a South Petherton innkeeper, Francis Pyke the postmaster of Crewkerne, William Gapper an illiterate yeoman' (Underdown 1973: 167–8). In Sussex most of the captains of the new militia were drawn from 'the minor gentry and aspiring townsmen' (Fletcher 1975: 295–6).

> Perhaps the greatest social change in Lancashire after the Civil War occurred in the county militia. Under Charles I it was almost an axiom that the militia officers should be recruited from the county elite. Thus between 1628 and 1642 all twenty-nine Lancashire militia officers held the status of esquire or above. But when the council of state reorganized the Lancashire militia in 1650 and appointed twenty-seven officers, only two of them belonged to the greater gentry. (Blackwood 1978: 85–6.)

Most of the rest were minor gentry, but ten were not even gentry.

Minor gentry, and even plebeians, took positions from which men of their status would previously have been generally excluded. That was because so many peers and greater gentry were royalists, neutrals or renegades from the parliamentarian cause, but that itself is highly significant of the social context of the revolution and revealing of the social bases of the parties. The lesser gentry who replaced greater gentry in the government of their counties were often men of some substance and local importance in their parishes, who had been on the fringes of power and had often held minor offices in local government before the war. It is characteristic of revolutions that they provide opportunities for such men, and indeed ambition for power may have led some of them to accept the new regime and profit from serving it (Clark 1977: 392–3). They were a minority of the lesser gentry and it does not follow that the lesser gentry as a whole supported the *coup d'état* of 1648–49 and the revolution, indeed far from it. Everitt believes that 'the vast majority' of 'the parochial gentry' in Kent 'were as antipathetic to the new regimes as were the greater county gentry'. Blackwood concludes from his study of the Lancashire gentry that 'while most republicans were perhaps lesser gentry, most lesser gentry were not republicans'. And those minor gentry who came to power as a result of the revolution were not necessarily radicals of any sort. (Everitt 1966: 296–7; Underdown 1971: 36, 307, 315–17, 327–8; Blackwood 1978: 73–4, 86–7, 100–1.)

Historians generally assert that the shift of power was not from one class to another but within a class, from the greater to the lesser gentry (Morrill 1982: 11–12; 1992: 99–101; Blackwood 1978: 86–7; Everitt 1966: 296–7). But since the hierarchy of status within the gentry and in society at large was regarded by contemporaries as so important for stability and order, the shift of political power from greater to lesser families was socially significant, and as Alan Smith points out: 'This was a very important shift in social power in the status-obsessed world of the mid-seventeenth century ...' (Smith, Alan G.R. 1984: 331–2, 348). Even more to the point, the gentry were not a class but a status grouping: the peers and greater gentry were a class – the ruling class, and so the shift of power was from the ruling class. In this context the overlap between the minor gentry and the yeomanry, as noted in Chapter 1, is very relevant. The men who took over power were leaders of the alliance of groups which supported parliament in the Civil War, and what is important is the source of their prominence, which often came from their religious zeal and the support of 'middle sort of people'.

The active supporters of the republic included minorities from different classes, according to Hutton, but a larger minority 'amongst the middle ranks, from parish gentry down through merchants and tradespeople to artisans ...' (Hutton 1990: 39, 79–80, 83). The general picture remains imprecise owing to varying definitions of the 'middle sort', and patchy due to the paucity of evidence, but recent research points towards the importance of the weighting towards the 'middle ranks' and 'the godly'. In Hampshire the regimes of the 1650s looked for active support to the 'godly' minority – Congregationalists, Baptists, and other radical sects (Coleby 1987: 74). In Cheshire the new governing group was allied with 'the better sort' of the parishes, 'the most religious and discreet inhabitants' (Morrill 1974: 239–41). A 'group of radical small squires' ruled in Glamorgan in the 1650s in cooperation with 'yeomen, husbandmen and rural tradesmen' of the 'parish elites' – 'the middling sort', which, says Stephen Roberts, is 'surely the best description of these people' (Roberts 1986: 226, 232–4, 245–7). Governing in the 1650s, according to the Cromwellian Major-General Goffe, had to depend on 'the middle sort of men' (Fletcher 1975: 308). John Morrill's observations on the agents of local government in the interregnum are suggestive:

> It seems likely that the bureaucracy of local government – the hordes of assessors, collectors, commissioners over and above the traditional officers of the civil parish (the constables, overseers and churchwardens) – spread responsibility more widely than ever before, especially among those groups on the margins of literacy. For the middling sort, the role of the grand jury at quarter sessions and assizes, assisting the justices and judges in the work of county government, may have been enhanced. In

Cheshire, for example, we find grand juries made up of substantial farmers and men in the grey area separating the gentry and the yeomanry criticizing the JPs as a whole for their failure to carry out their duties properly and even telling the assize judges who ought to be added to the commission of the peace. (Morrill 1992: 110.)

Everitt's judgement that the revolution proved that England could only be governed by the greater gentry has been challenged by John Morrill and Ann Hughes. (Everitt 1966: chs 8, 9; Morrill 1974: ch. 6; Hughes 1987: ch. 7.) A new ruling class emerged, selected from among minor gentry, yeomen, merchants, army officers and radical clergy, and it governed the country effectively in the 1650s, but it lacked the economic power and social base to sustain its position permanently.

Success and Failure of the Left

Under the wing of the Levellers the first women's movement appeared. In 1649 they organised their own campaign in support of the Leveller leaders who were arrested and imprisoned by the new republican regime. They drew up a petition and sent copies of it 'to all parts about London, to desire that all those women that are approvers thereof should subscribe it, which accordingly many did, and delivered in their subscriptions to certain women appointed in every ward and division to receive the same'. They canvassed women at services in the sectarian churches, where 'in some places many signed, in other places none at all, and in some places it was disputed'. They collected the signatures of 10,000 women, so it was said, and urged their supporters to accompany the petition to Westminster, which several hundred women did and returned day after day clamouring to have it heard. When the House of Commons refused to listen and told them to go home 'and look after your own business, and meddle with your housewifery', they declared that they had 'an equal interest with the men of this nation' in its laws and liberties and against injustices and cruelties. They claimed the right as women to make their views known publicly on political and religious matters, but they did not call for votes for women, and they did not challenge directly the patriarchal organisation of the family and society (Higgins 1973: 200–5, 216–17).

The Levellers were founders of modern democracy in their struggle to make government dependent on the consent of the people and to decentralise power. But in ethos and tactics their movement was geared for protest rather than achieving power. Generally they did not involve themselves directly in the struggles of peasants to defend their rights or of artisans to protect their livelihoods, and so they failed to mobilise the masses. (Wootton 1991: 415–16; Walter 1991: 120–2; Carlin 1994: 253–4.) They did not grapple with the problem that extremes of wealth and poverty in a highly inegalitarian society made effective democratic control by the mass of the people unrealisable. Their hopes for a more democratic state could not be achieved so long as the aristocracy retained its vast estates and its power to make the people dependent and deferential. The big landlords, rich merchants and wealthy farmers controlled the economy and society by means of their ownership of the means of production and their exploitation of the labour of the people, who were being reduced to semi-proletarians by loss of possession of the means of production in the form of land or instruments of manufacture. The Levellers had little or nothing to say to them.

There emerged in 1649 on the left of the Levellers, however, a movement of 'true levellers' or Diggers as they were nicknamed, who were founders of socialism in that they recognised the economic imperatives of true democracy. They protested against private property, the market economy and waged labour. They tried to establish communes on the uncultivated common and wastelands as models of a society in which there would be no landlords, no rents to pay, no one would have to work for wages, but all would own the land in common, cultivate it together and share equitably its produce. Such communes appeared in ten or so places, including Cobham in Surrey, Enfield in Middlesex, and Wellingborough in Northamptonshire, but only small numbers were involved and their existence was brief before being crushed by the violence of landlords, wealthy farmers and lawcourts.

The aim of the Diggers was not to opt out of society but to revolutionise it. They had supported parliament in the Civil War and rejoiced at the abolition of the monarchy and the House of Lords and the proclamation of 'a free commonwealth'. But they knew that the mass of the people were still not free: they were oppressed by landlords and lawyers and clergy; they still had to pay rents and fines to landlords or to work for starvation wages, to pay tithes to the clergy who upheld the existing social and economic order, to pay taxes to support an army which was increasingly used to suppress popular protests, and to suffer injustices because they could not afford the costs of legal proceedings. '... England cannot be a free commonwealth till this bondage be taken away. You have taken away the king; you have taken away the House of Lords; now step two steps further and take away the power of lords of manors, and of tything priests, and the intolerable oppressions of judges ... .' Only the rich have real freedom, the poor will not be truly free until they have 'the land of their nativity for their livelihood, freed from entanglements of lords, lords of manors, and landlords, which are our taskmasters'. The Diggers did not intend to provide only the model of an alternative society but to raise the political consciousness of the masses and to inspire them to emancipate themselves by direct action. They called upon tenants to refuse to pay rents and upon workers to withdraw their labour, so that large estates and big farms would be unable to continue to operate and their owners would have to accept the new social and economic order (Manning 1992: 109–32). The Diggers, however, did not solve the problems of the political framework for economic democracy.

Cromwell led the defence of the republic against royalist threats from Scotland and Ireland, which were conquered and subordinated to the English state. In the 1640s he had put himself at the head of radical elements, though often hesitantly and ambiguously, but from 1649 he joined with religious and political leaders of the new republican regime, and with senior officers of the army, to defeat challenges from the Levellers and the left wing of the revolution. But supporters of the republic still expected that it would lead to radical reforms, particularly of tithes and of the legal system. The officers became frustrated at the failure of such reforms to emerge from the 'Rump Parliament' which had continued in power since the purge of December 1648. They forcibly dissolved it in 1653 and installed Cromwell as head of the government with the title of Lord Protector.

Cromwell was committed to reform of the legal system, being a persistent critic of the complexity, slowness and costs of legal proceedings, as well as of the imposition of the death penalty for petty thefts. But unable or unwilling to overcome the resistance of the lawyers to radical change he achieved very little. He defended the liberty of 'the godly' 'to worship God according to their own light and consciences', but would not extend this to 'popery', prelacy, or denial of the divinity of Christ or of the authority of the Bible, and insisted that the civil authorities retain the power to restrict it if it became, in their eyes, a cover for sedition, blasphemy, or immorality. He was not himself identified with any sect and he sought to prevent any one religious group imposing itself on the nation as the only faith to which all must conform, and providing the Presbyterians gave up that ambition he was prepared to number them among 'the godly'. He established a loose national church which he hoped would unite Presbyterians, Congregationalists and Baptists. He defended the parochial structure and to this end insisted that compulsory maintenance must continue to be paid to the ministers of parishes, accepting that this should still be by tithes until some other form of provision could be found by the state. The crucial division in the 1650s came between those who rejected any form of national church and those who wished to retain some

form of national church, and Cromwell fell decisively into the
latter camp. Still more importantly the regimes of the 1650s
defended the old social order and hierarchy against radical challenges.
Again Cromwell took the lead: 'A nobleman, a gentleman, a
yeoman – the distinction of these – that is a good interest of the
nation, and a great one', he said. He tried to reconcile the old ruling
class to his regime: 'We would keep up the nobility and gentry ...'.
He enhanced his power by posing as the barrier to social revolution
and gained acquiescence from the middling as well as the upper
ranks of society by exaggerating the threat from radicals to private
property and to 'reducing all to an equality' (Hill 1970: 150, 154,
187, 205). But in the end his regime rested upon his control of the
army, whose officers gained wealth, position and power from the
revolution.

CHAPTER 7

Revolution and Counter-Revolution

> ... The question is whether a sword shall prevail ... or if England shall return again to be governed by parliaments ...
>
> EARL OF LAUDERDALE, 1660

Revolution Renewed

After the death of Cromwell on 3 September 1658 his son Richard attempted to continue the Protectorate but was overthrown by a military *coup d'état* on 21 April 1659. The driving force behind this came from the junior officers and the whole radical movement. It expressed a renewed revolutionary momentum. The officers recalled the Long Parliament in the shape of the purged House of Commons that ruled from 1649 to 1653, nicknamed the 'Rump Parliament'. The Cromwellian Protectorate and its supporters were repudiated and the slogan of the regenerated revolution was defence of the 'Good Old Cause', which was defined as government without 'a single person' (i.e. Protector), king, or House of Lords.

Inhabitants of Southwark, industrial suburb of London and radical centre, declared on 27 April that they had taken up arms for parliament in the Civil War

> ... in judgement and conscience for the fundamental laws of the land, the native rights and freedoms of the people (which neither king-craft, nor protector-craft, neither age nor time can obliterate) and fought it out with those abettors of monarchy to an absolute conquest both of that Norman cause and family, restoring the people to the freedom of a commonwealth ... without king and House of Lords ... .

They reminded the officers and soldiers of the army:

> ... you are not the army of monarchy, to settle the government in a single person either of the old or new family, but the popular army, the army of a free state, to settle the people in full possession and enjoyment of the fundamental laws and liberties of England ... .
>
> We need not now remind you of the *Solemn Engagement of the Army* at Newmarket and Triploe heath, nor of the *Agreement*

of the People upon the fundamentals of English freedom ... , nor the petition of 11 September 1648, owned by you ... , nor your many other remonstrances, declarations, vows, and promises to the people ... .

Radicals, however, did not rest upon the formal institutional definition of the 'Good Old Cause' as government without king and House of Lords, for what that meant to them was the sovereignty of the people. As some watermen of London said:

Of old time indeed our parliaments have been intermixed and clogged with kingship and peerage, and though owned and of long continuance, yet were they of great abuse and violation to the just rights of the people ... neither king nor Lords being any part of the true parliaments of England, but an imposed power upon them from the interest of the old Norman sword; a true parliament being the representative of the people ... neither king nor Lords being chosen or representing either county, city, or borough, but merely as unnatural wens and bunches upon that authority, the evils whereof this nation had felt through all succession of times, the over-balance of those families proving fatal to the whole, multiplying miseries and calamities upon us at mere will and pleasure, till the same at last (extending too far) broke forth into an absolute war ... .

Henry Stubbe, in *An Essay in Defence of the Good Old Cause* (1659), explained:

And however some may say that it was none of the old cause to assert any proper sovereignty in the people, yet I must tell them that the vindications of the parliament against the papers of the king then in being show us that such a sovereignty was presupposed, and, if it were not the old cause, it was the foundation thereof ... .

Petitions and manifestos reasserted the Levellers' doctrine that the people were 'the original of all just power' and that ''tis the first principle of a people's liberty, that they shall not be bound but by their own consent, and this our ancestors left to England as its undoubted right ...'.

The 78 survivors of the purged parliament of 1649–53, restored now to power at Westminster, could hardly be regarded as representing the people of England, but the expectation of the radicals was that they would establish the foundations of a 'free state', by providing for a succession of parliaments, automatically elected and dissolved at regular intervals. The agonising dilemma of radicals was that in theory they asserted the sovereignty of the people but in practice they could not trust the people to uphold the 'Good

Old Cause'. The crucial question, endlessly debated, was who would be eligible to elect and be elected. The exclusion of royalists was common ground, but frequently the logic was to define eligibility in terms of adherence to the 'Good Old Cause'. Theory and practice could be reconciled by redefining 'the people'. A Leveller tract – *Lilburne's Ghost, with a whip in one hand to scourge tyrants out of authority, and balm in the other to heal the sores of our (as yet) corrupt state* (1659) (Lilburne had died in 1657) – spelt it out to parliament:

> And as you ought to be careful of the persons to be elected, so you ought to be as careful of the persons electing, who ought to be such as have made contribution of their purses, strength and counsels, to manage the cause for the liberty and freedom of the people; for in this case those only ought to be reckoned the people, the rest having by a traitorous engagement, compliance, neutrality, or apostasy, endeavoured to destroy the people, and by consequence have forfeited their rights and membership of free people, are no longer to be called patriots, but parties in faction, having acted against the declared interest of the commonwealth.

The issues of liberty of conscience and religious toleration were of fundamental importance to all radicals. Most of them were members of the Protestant sects who had partly or wholly broken away from the Church of England – Congregationalists, Baptists, Quakers, Fifth Monarchists (millenarians preparing for the imminent Second Coming of Christ) – and they were acutely conscious of being relatively small and often unpopular minorities. This shaped their attitudes towards the constitution and system of government, for to allow power to the opponents of the 'Good Old Cause' would be to give it to the opponents of liberty of conscience and religious toleration, and indeed they had as much to fear from Presbyterian parliamentarians as from episcopalian royalists. At one level was the demand that 'tender consciences' that could not conform to the established church should be permitted to worship in their own separate congregations according to their own lights. Petitions from the lord mayor, aldermen and common council of London; from 'many inhabitants in and about London'; from young men and apprentices of Southwark; and from Kent and Bedfordshire, urged 'that provision may be made' that those 'of different persuasions in matters of faith and worship, may be equally protected and encouraged ...'. But all these petitions put some restriction on this freedom, confining it to 'good and peaceable people', or to 'those that fear God and walk holy according to the rule of God's Word', or to 'such who live peaceably in godliness and honesty'. In fact the radicals were constantly divided over where to draw the line and how far religious toleration should extend. The officers of the army restricted it to those who believed in the Trinity and accepted the Bible as the Word of God. They excluded from it Roman Catholics and episcopalians, and 'such as shall practise or hold forth licentiousness or profaneness under the profession of religion ...'. The author of *The Humble Desires of a Free Subject* (1659) insisted on belief in the Trinity and excluded all those that 'hold forth anything that shall tend to blasphemy, or profaneness, or is repugnant to the truth contained in the Word of God'. The author of *The Grand Concernment of England Ensured* (1659) would not tolerate those who denied the divinity of Christ, or who did not accept that the Bible was the rule of faith and conduct, or who thought that Sunday was not special; and indeed the freedom he allowed was so narrow as be restricted to those who 'fear God, and are sound in the substantials of Christianity, howsoever they may differ in those things that the Scriptures are not so express and clear in, and in modes and forms of worship and discipline ...', so long as 'they destroy not the doctrines or life of Christianity, and live peaceably in the state ...'. All these approaches were based on the assumption that there were certain fundamentals of religion which the state must have the power to impose on the nation and to prohibit contrary views.

At a more profound level was the old Leveller argument against all coercion in religion: truth rested upon the understanding and conscience of the individual, but individuals did not agree about the truth, and no one had the right to impose his conception of the truth by force upon another; therefore when the people came together to form a state they did not have the right collectively to delegate to it the power to compel men in religion because they did not have that right individually. This underpinned a position of fundamental importance in the revolution – the rejection of the traditional assumption that the stability of the state and society depended on unity in religion, and the acceptance of the idea of the separation of church and state. The Leveller tract *Lilburne's Ghost* declared that parliament should 'have nothing to do in matters of religion'. A Baptist manifesto said 'that no magistrate has received power from Christ to punish for, or to compel any to this or that form of religion'. Edward Byllynge, a Quaker, protested 'that the magistrate has no coercive power whatsoever in matters of religion, faith, or worship ...'. And a manifesto of Fifth Monarchists insisted 'that the magistrate intermeddle not in the matters of Christ's church or spiritual concernments ...', and demanded that 'the rulers over men for ever forbear to impose ... any form of worship'. This manifesto rejected a national church and parishes and the compulsory maintenance of ministers by tithes. The issue became, not how far dissent should be allowed from the national church, but whether there should be a national church at all. With the growth of the sects religion was developing *de facto* into a pluralistic and voluntaristic system, in which individuals, instead of attending their parish church with their neighbours, selected amongst a variety of congregations one where they found like-minded spirits (a free market in religion to match the free market of capitalism).

Radicals proclaimed that liberty of conscience and freedom of worship were civil rights inseparable from the foundation of a 'free state'. *A Commonwealth or Nothing: or, Monarchy and Oligarchy proved parallel in tyranny* (1659) held that the fatal error of the sects in the early 1650s was to be persuaded that religious liberty could be separated from civil liberty. William Sprigge argued that without civil liberty there could be no religious liberty, and without religious liberty there could be no civil liberty. The thesis of another tract was evident from its title – *England's Settlement, upon the two solid foundations of the People's civil and religious liberties* (1659):

> The other main basis or pillar, that must uphold the great fabric of this state, to make it stand firm and sure, is the spiritual liberty of the people as they are Christians; which consists in this, that no person professing faith in Christ be molested or oppressed in his conscience for his judgement in matters of religion, or in things relating to the worship and service of God.

' ... Where civil liberty is entire, it includes liberty of conscience', wrote the Leveller leader William Bray in *A Plea for the People's Good Old Cause* (1659), 'and where liberty of conscience is entire, it includes civil liberty; they are the inseparable RIGHT of the people .... Liberty of conscience must have security under any government, or else the opposers thereof will descend into an inevitability tyranny ... if either major or minor part in a nation deprives the others of liberty of conscience, it is tyranny'. Toleration of differences in religion and protection against intolerant majorities or minorities would have been giant steps towards freedom, still not accomplished in the twentieth century.

Closely related to the question of religious freedom, and central to the programme of the radicals, was the issue of tithes – the system of taxation by which the national church was supported – and it was raised in a stream of petitions and pamphlets. Just as the advocates of liberty of conscience were divided between those who wished to retain a national church but with a degree of freedom for those unwilling to conform to it, and those who wanted to eliminate any form of national church, so the critics of tithes were divided between supporters of a national church that nevertheless desired to replace tithes by a fairer and more acceptable system of taxation for the maintenance of its ministers, and those who opposed a national church and so any form of compulsory levy to support the clergy. There were two main grounds for the abolition of tithes: one was that sectarians should not be forced to contribute towards the maintenance of ministers whose churches they did not attend; and the other was that they were 'a very great oppression' especially on farmers and a hindrance to agricultural improvements.

Arguments against tithes showed a concern with agrarian grievances, and so did the campaign in the summer of 1659 against the obligations and insecurity of many copyhold tenants (their tenure was regulated by the customs of the manor from which they held their land). Petitions from Buckinghamshire, Bedfordshire and Hertfordshire called for the abolition of copyhold tenure and pamphlets urged its conversion into freehold. But radicals tended to devote less attention to agrarian questions than to grievances against the legal system; in the latter case calling for codification and simplification of the law and decentralisation of the courts from Westminster to the localities, where cases would be decided by judges and juries chosen by local people.

It seemed that what Ronald Hutton calls 'the second English Revolution' was about to take place. Radicals dominated the press and petitions, and their renewed vigour, confidence and urgency was backed by 'a larger and more widely distributed basis of popular support' than in 1649, as the result of the expansion of the sects in the intervening years (Hutton 1990: 121–2). But the Rump Parliament consisted of the same people as had resisted the radicals in 1649, and they were no more willing to submit to radical proposals in 1659. The Rump was ejected by another military *coup d'état* on 13 October 1659, but the officers could not agree on what to put in its place, and the army and the radicals were both split by the coup, some supporting it but many opposing it, and this proved fatal to the revolution.

Popular Revolt 1659–1660

Repeatedly throughout the period of the revolution there were riots against enclosures, but the revolutionaries far from opposing enclosures generally supported them. The growth of capitalist agriculture had led the bigger farmers to promote enclosures. 'In the middle of the seventeenth century, opinion amongst the "middle sort of people" showed a decisive shift in favour of enclosure ... .' Walter Blith, for example, was the son of a yeoman in the Forest of Arden in Warwickshire: he was a strong supporters of parliament in the Civil War and a captain in its army and a holder of minor offices under the republic. 'In about 1650 he acquired an estate at Cotesbach in Leicestershire and entitled himself "gentleman".' About the same time he published *The English Improver*, in which he advocated enclosures, provided that the legitimate interests of the poor in unenclosed commons were recognised (Manning 1992: 77–8). 'Blith's proposals were rooted in actual agricultural practice in the Forest of Arden where, in the first half of the seventeenth century, middling sort yeomen and husbandmen were active enclosers and improvers.' Buchanan Sharp suggests that Blith embodied 'the economic aspirations of the middling sort' (Sharp 1992: 263–4). The most violent resistance to enclosures took place in the forests and fens and was put down by the regimes of the 1650s employing the army (Sharp 1980: 250–4; Lindley 1982: 161–87). Alienation between the officers of the army and peasants with grievances against enclosures was exemplified by a riot at Enfield in the summer of 1659.

When the Cromwellian regime disposed of certain royal forests, it sold part of Enfield Chase in Middlesex to a number of senior army officers. The latter included George Joyce, now a colonel, who as the agent of army democracy seized the king in 1647 and as the agent of Cromwellian rule expropriated the rights of peasants in 1658, thus exhibiting the two faces of the English Revolution. The Chase was open land, some of it wooded, on which the inhabitants of Enfield and Edmonton had ancient rights of common to pasture cattle and to take wood. The officers proceeded to divide up their part of the Chase into discrete farms and enclose them, erect houses and outbuildings, plough up the pastures and plant corn. The inhabitants protested that their 'just rights' were 'forced from them by strong hand', and in that part of the Chase left to them they could not maintain anything like their previous numbers of cattle. Seizing the opportunity of the collapse of the Protectorate they broke down the hedges and filled in the ditches around the enclosures and drove their cattle into the growing corn. Some of them were indicted for riot at the quarter sessions but acquitted by the jury. Soldiers were sent to protect the houses and corn of the purchasers. One file of fifteen commanded by a sergeant encountered a crowd armed with pitchforks, scythes, axes and long poles. The soldiers fired on the countrymen, several were wounded and two died. The people fought back and, while the soldiers were reloading their muskets, overpowered them, fatally wounding the sergeant and hurting nine others, who were made prisoners and handed over to the law. The people proceeded to destroy all the corn, burn stacks of wood, demolish houses and barns, and drive away the servants and workmen of the purchasers. Both sides complained to parliament and the sheriff and JPs persuaded the people to disperse while they awaited the adjudication of parliament, but troops of horse were at hand to prevent further rioting (Pam 1977: 10–12; Sharp 1992: 267–8). Whereas in the enclosure riots of the 1640s, such as those at Gillingham described in Chapter

5, the enemy appeared as the king or parliament or both, now it appeared as the army. Peasant discontent was aggravated by the revolution and not harnessed in support of the revolution.

The English Revolution was ushered in by an economic depression and a panic fear of 'papists' in 1641–42; it was ushered out by an economic depression and a panic fear of 'sectaries' in 1659–60.

In 1659–60 numerous tracts and petitions complained about the depression of trade, increased unemployment, higher food prices, and the sufferings of the poor. The winter of 1659–60 was very severe, there was frost and snow continuously from early November to early February, which deepened the depression and meant a 'hard time for poor, who pine exceedingly nipped with want and penury' (Josselin 1976: 435, 454–9). It was not a good time to argue, as some radicals did, that a 'free state' was better for trade than a monarchy, and the question put by *The Unhappy Marksman: or, twenty-three queries* (1659) was very apposite: 'Whether the name of a free state be able in a dear year to feed poor people with bread and porridge?'. But while the economic depression did have an influence in popular disorders and weakened support for the republic during the winter of 1659–60, it did not lead directly to the restoration of the monarchy.

The toleration of the sects and the entry of sectaries into local offices and local militias produced a popular backlash. Barry Reay argues that 'the events of 1659 may be compared with the fear of Catholic plots in England in the early 1640s or the Great Fear in France over a century later. It was *grande peur* and fear of Catholics in reverse, however. The generalised suspicion and terror encouraged by pulpit and print stimulated reaction, not revolution.' Charles II, he believes, was swept back onto the throne by a wave of reaction against the toleration of the sects, notably the Fifth Monarchists, Quakers and Baptists (Reay 1985: ch. 5). This is exaggerated, but fear of the sects was fanned by rumour in 1659–60 and contributed to anxiety and unsettlement.

A warning was spread in the streets of London on 6 June 1659:

> The Fifth Monarchy men are armed, officered, and every way in readiness, upon the word given them, to surprise and suppress the army, to fire the city, and to massacre all considerable people of all sorts, whom they suspect averse to what they impiously designed.

BEWARE TUESDAY NEXT; WE SAY, BEWARE

The Baptists protested against 'wicked and devilish' lies that they 'had lately gotten knives, hooked knives, and the like, and great store of arms ... intending to cut the throats of such as were contrary minded to us in matters of religion, and that many such knives, and arms, for the carrying on some secret design have been found in some of our houses by search ...'.

The clearest examples of panic come from the summer of 1659 in Devon and Somerset, where rumours spread 'that Baptists and Quakers were joined together to cut the throats of all the ministers and magistrates of those parts'. The contemporary newspaper *Mercurius politicus* gives a vivid account of the popular panic at Tiverton on the night of 14 July (it was the second largest town in Devon, a centre of the cloth industry, home to religious radicals since the 1620s and strongly parliamentarian in the Civil War: attitudes in such a place in 1659 would be significant for the survival of the 'Good Old Cause'):

> Neighbours roused up each other out of their beds, crying pitifully one to another, Take Arms! Take Arms! else they would have their throats cut in their beds. And when they came forth of their houses, and asked the reason of this hurly-burly and fear, the common reply and general cry was, that the Baptists and Quakers were joined together, and intended that night to cut the throats of the ministers, and all the godly people, whereupon some (being wiser than the rest) returned to their beds, as judging there was no cause of fear. But others ... took arms, and walked through the town. The cry for a while increased and grew higher and higher ... They had an intent to have beaten their drums, and rung the bells at midnight, but some persuaded to the contrary, which was a great mercy to a few Baptists living in that town, for it is probable, had such a thing been done, the rude multitude in their rage ... would have plucked their houses down upon them. But they did only set a guard about their houses (which were ten or twelve families) ... .

The commotion subsided as the report was found to be false. There is not much evidence of similar panics elsewhere, and even here not everybody believed the rumour, and the reaction was restrained within bounds.

There is, however, much evidence of popular hostility towards the sects. From early 1660 onwards mobs in various places assaulted Quakers, Baptists and Fifth Monarchists, and the mob which attacked Quakers in Harwich cried 'the king is now coming, who will hang or banish you all' (Reay 1985: 99; Hutton 1987: 99). County petitions from Leicestershire and Northamptonshire, for example, called for 'the true Protestant religion' to be 'professed and defended, all heresies, sects and schisms discountenanced and suppressed ...'; and petitioners in Kent said that they were more concerned about the 'prodigious growth of blasphemies, heresies and schism' than about the 'total decay and subversion of trade'.

But the tide did not flow entirely towards greater intolerance, for Warwickshire and Gloucestershire urged that 'liberty be allowed to tender consciences'. Reaction against the sects did weaken the republic but it was not sufficient in itself to bring about the restoration of the monarchy.

Material deprivation and fear of the sects flowed into a popular campaign for a 'free parliament', which could mean either the readmission of the members purged in December 1648, or a general election for a new parliament. General Monck persuaded and coerced the English army in Scotland to oppose the coup of 13 October 1659 and he became the focus of the campaign for a 'free parliament'. But it was that campaign rather than the intervention of Monck and his army which was the turning-point of revolution into counter-revolution.

During November 1659 petitions to the common council were being organised in London. The agitation originated, as in 1647, among the young men and apprentices, and the seamen and watermen. The economic situation was very much in the minds of the petitioners: *The Humble Petition and Address of the Seamen and Watermen* spoke of 'the extraordinary decay of merchandise, trade ...', and *The Most Humble Petition and Address of divers young men on the behalf of themselves and the apprentices* said that the 'general decay of trading ... does exceed the worst of former times ...'. The seamen and watermen were also worried about the growth of religious radicalism and political instability, speaking of 'the extraordinary decay of ... religion, justice, piety, and inundation of all sorts of apprehensions ... tumults, sects heresies, blasphemies, alterations of government, and destructive confusions ...'. The young men and apprentices desired 'that the ministry may be countenanced and encouraged, the universities upheld and maintained ...', which meant they were against the abolition of tithes. Both sets of petitioners saw the only solution to be a 'free parliament': '... to settle the government, redress the grievances, restore the peace, merchandise, trade, and navigation of this nation' (according to the seamen and watermen); '... the most probable means under God to establish the true Protestant religion, reform the laws, secure our liberties and preserve our lives and outward concernments, to promote learning and encourage virtue ...', to see 'the army satisfied, their arrears paid, and trading restored' (according to the young men and apprentices). These petitions were by no means wholly reactionary or counter-revolutionary.

On 1 December the provisional government, set up by the officers since the October coup, banned the petition of the young men and apprentices and prohibited them from signing it. On 3 December the lord mayor of London ordered heads of household to see that 'their sons and servants' did not take part in 'any unlawful attempts or designs'. But every evening multitudes of young men and apprentices flocked to a house in Cannon Street to sign the petition, and it was said that 20,000 signatures were collected. In defiance of the ban it was decided to present the petition to the common council on 5 December. The provisional government sent regiments of horse and foot to maintain order in the city and the Sergeant-at-Arms to make proclamation that the petition was illegal. The soldiers found 'great multitudes of the ordinary sort of people were gathered together in the streets, and the shops shut up ...'. Their way was blocked by large numbers of young men and apprentices playing football in the street – no doubt to conceal their real purpose of supporting the petition being delivered at the Guildhall by their comrades. According to accounts in the contemporary newspapers:

> ... a head of apprentices gathered together, and heating one another at the exercise of football, they were desired by the troopers to forbear that sport which interrupted them in their expedition, and served only to draw more numbers together, contrary to the late order of the lord mayor and common council; but the apprentices unwilling to depart, did fall to a hooping and a hollering, and some commotion there was ... .

Colonel Hewson came up with his regiment of foot and began to clear the streets: '... several stones were cast at them from the tops of houses, and elsewhere, and great shoutings, and pressing upon the rear, insomuch that some of the musketeers faced about and fired, killing six or seven, and wounding nineteen or twenty ...'. Other accounts gave the killed variously at two or three and three or four, with 20 or 30 wounded.

The common council, in contradiction of the order of the provisional government, received the petition and appointed a committee to take it into speedy consideration, and, in view of the bloodshed in the streets, sent to the commander-in-chief of the army, General Fleetwood, to have the soldiers withdrawn from the city. The lord mayor and sheriffs addressed the crowds and informed them of the actions of the common council, which were sufficient to persuade them to disperse, much to the relief of the older and wealthier citizens: '... the substantial and sober body of the city ... foreseeing the fatal consequences that must ensue, if the reins of government were once let loose to the multitude, gave no countenance to that rude and tumultuous proceeding', recorded *Mercurius Politicus*.

There was bitter anger amongst the apprentices at the killing of their comrades, and this was shared by many of the citizens: '... those infamous murders committed, but Monday last, upon our unarmed friends ...'; '... that execrable Monday (sacred to the eternal infamy of this city) ...'; '... the mercenary soldiers did murder, slay, and wound many of us, only to prevent our peaceable way of petitioning you for such things as concerned the safety of this city, and well-being of this nation ...'; '... that sad and miserable distraction and confusion which happened in this famous city on Monday the 5th instant, and the several notorious murders then committed, all which we conceive have been of late chiefly occasioned by the interruption of the parliament, the 13th of October last ...'. The young men and apprentices set up a gibbet from which they hanged Hewson in effigy, and built snowmen in his likeness with halters about their necks. A coroner's inquest found the killing of the apprentices wilful murder and the grand jury drew up an indictment against Hewson who was alleged to have given the order to shoot (Harris 1987: 42–5). Popular hostility towards the military and the provisional government was intensified, and the soldiers themselves were demoralised by their situation and alienated from the provisional government.

Anger began to be channelled into political organisation. On the day after the killings a pamphlet, *A Free Parliament proposed by the City to the Nation*, propounded an 'Engagement':

> We the free-born people of England, having for many years last past, been subjected in our consciences, persons, and estates, to the arbitrary and lawless impositions of ambitious and cruel-minded men; and finding ourselves at present in danger to be irrecoverably lost ... without the seasonable mediation of a free parliament: We do declare that we will by all lawful means endeavour the convening of it ...; we do further engage ... that if any person or persons whatsoever shall presume to oppose us, or to impose upon us any other government, inconsistent with, or destructive to the constitution of parliaments, we will prosecute him, or them, as the betrayers of the people's rights, and subverters of the fundamental laws of the English nation.

It was said that thousands in the city signed this engagement and it was commended to the nation as a whole. Adopting tactics which the Levellers had proposed in 1649, the authors advocated a campaign of refusal to pay taxes until a 'free parliament' was convened, and each county to choose two representatives to liaise with the Londoners.

By the convening of a 'free parliament' the apprentices meant the holding of a general election, with the same restrictions on who could vote and be chosen that existed before the Civil War. But *The Representation of Divers Citizens of London*, delivered to Fleetwood and his officers on 6 December, contented itself with urging that the Rump Parliament be allowed to sit again. It said that no doubt the army's intention in discontinuing that parliament on 13 October was to settle 'those things so long contended for, by a speedier hand than that of the parliament (of whose grave, slow pace you were impatient), expecting thereby to give full satisfaction to all your friends and adherents, to the uniting them the firmer to you'. But the army's action had dissatisfied its friends and encouraged its enemies, and the only way to correct this was to let that parliament resume its trust 'in settling the distracted affairs of this common-wealth, and making provision for future parliaments ...'. On 9 December an appeal to the lord mayor said that as a result of 'Bloody Monday'

> ... the distractions and decay of trade are like to grow every day worse and worse, unless some speedy way and means be found out, to put a stop to the torrent of the rampant sword, that so the parliament may again return with safety to the free exercise and discharge of their trust in settling the government of these nations, upon true and sure foundations of a free state and commonwealth; by which all the good people of these nations, both as men and Christians, may enjoy their common and equal rights and freedoms, both in their persons and estates, which undoubtedly is, and will be, the only, speediest, and most probable way and means, for a full and free trade once more to flourish in these nations, to the encouragement of all art, labour and industry, the only glory and sinews of a good and well-ordered commonwealth.

The soldiers in London repudiated Fleetwood and his clique of officers and restored the Rump Parliament on 26 December. The common council of London, however, was not satisfied and voted for a 'free parliament'. The return of the Rump was rapidly overtaken by the campaign for a 'free parliament' which had been triggered by the action of the London apprentices. The apprentices of Bristol declared their intention of following the example of the apprentices of London, who were also supported by petitions from Gloucestershire, Suffolk and Kent.

In January 1660 the meeting of the quarter sessions at Exeter was made the occasion for the gentry of Devon to gather to discuss what they should do in the present situation. A letter of 14 January published in the newspaper *The Parliamentary Intelligencer* described how they 'found divers of the inhabitants groaning under high oppressions and a general defect of trade, to the utter ruin of many, and fear of the like to others (which is as visible in the whole county) ...'. It gives an illuminating account of the genesis of a riot and the control of popular disorder:

> ... whilst they were in consultation, a distracted man ran through the streets, crying out 'A Free Parliament! A Free Parliament!',

a multitude of boys about ten or twelve years old following him, they called him 'captain', and he them his soldiers, and thus they trooped it about for some time in the city. In some while after, it ceased to be boys' play, many of the lusty young fellows of the city gather together, to them flock the necessitous people, who by reason of the great decay of trade, the hardness of the winter, and the soldiers' free-quarter (which has eaten up that relief that was usually bestowed on those poor creatures) are very numerous. These kept up the mad man's cry too. The mayor alarmed by this uproar, sent to all parts of the city enjoining them to repair everyone to his own habitation, but they made too much noise themselves to hear another speak, and were too many to yield to one. The mayor seeing his commands slighted went a second time to them with some of the magistrates, but they were likewise too few, there was a louder noise than theirs, the poor men's bellies cried to them and they to their magistrates, we want bread, and choose rather to perish by the sword than famine. The mayor perceiving that his and his brethren's authority could prevail but little in appeasing the people's fury, bethought himself to attempt that by policy, which he could not, at least without very much bloodshed, have done by force.

He acquiesced in the apprentices and young men taking control of the gates of the city, which they locked and guarded against anyone going in or out. This had the advantage, from the mayor's point-of-view, of dividing the crowd into smaller groups, which he infiltrated with 'several sober prudent men, who mixed themselves with the rabble' and took command of the guards at the gates and 'kept them waking and active all night'. 'On the morning the mayor and magistrates went again about the city, using both commands and entreaties to them, that they might repair to their own houses.' Exhausted by a sleepless night, they were tamer now and obeyed. But that afternoon there reached the city a troop of horse reputed to contain Baptists, 'a generation of men not so well esteemed by many of good repute in these parts'. A hostile crowd gathered but was restrained by the vigorous action of the mayor, magistrates and county gentry. The county gentry subscribed a declaration demanding the readmission to parliament of those members purged in December 1648, and the filling by by-elections of those seats left vacant by death. This gave some satisfaction to the citizens. 'Never till now have I known such a tumult in this city ...', wrote an inhabitant, and one of the gentry said that these disorders 'were no small trouble and disturbance to us ...'. The story of the Exeter riot contains all the elements of the crisis of the winter of 1659–60: economic depression, fear of sectaries, demand for a 'free parliament', and the prominent role of the apprentices. The maintenance of order this winter was coming to be predicated on the restoration of the purged MPs or the election of a new parliament.

The popular movement that developed during the winter of 1659–60, though not radical, may not properly be labelled 'reactionary' or 'counter-revolutionary', but be regarded as a continuation of the revolution which began in 1640. Christopher Hill points out that 'the landslide of 1660, like that of 1640, was for a restoration of "free parliaments" and of the law at least as much as of the king ...' (Hill 1984: 322). The slogan of the movement was a 'free parliament' and monarchy was not mentioned. John T. Evans, however, maintains that the movement in Norwich and Norfolk 'must be interpreted as thinly-veiled support for the restoration of the Stuarts ...' (Evans 1979: 223–5). But Ann Hughes comments on the movement in Warwickshire that it was not fuelled by a 'headlong or straightforward rush in the county towards royalist enthusiasm' (Hughes 1987: 330–2). Tim Harris concludes from his examination of the petitions and tumults in London:

> Clearly there was much genuine hostility towards army rule in late 1659 amongst the tradesmen, apprentices and labourers ... But this unrest should not be seen as evidence of a conservative reaction. The rhetoric employed was both libertarian and populist, the people threatening to take direct action themselves to preserve what they perceived to be their 'rights and liberties'. The explicit call was not for a restoration of monarchy, but for a return to parliamentary forms of government.

The provisional government, of course, alleged that the tumults in London were 'promoted and designed' by cavaliers, who 'have been the chief actors in and abettors of them, although they have endeavoured to colour the same under the pretence and name of apprentices (some of which have been cunningly seduced and instigated by them) ...'. But Harris judges that this allegation was probably without foundation. An attempt by royalist agents to persuade the apprentices to rise in support of Charles II proved unsuccessful (Harris 1987: 45–6).

A huge campaign of meetings, declaration and petitions extended through the provinces for the readmission of the purged MPs or for a new parliament, and historians have assumed that this implied support for the restoration of the king (Woolrych 1980: 160–1; Aylmer 1986: 195–6). But it is by no means certain that this was how most people saw it at the time. What is striking is that the rhetoric of this campaign was parliamentarian, populist and libertarian, and that it expressed the ideology which was the dynamic of the revolution – that power should ascend from the people, and that government should be by the consent of the people. A 'free parliament' was 'the only bulwark and defence of our liberties', proclaimed petitioners from Gloucestershire. '... The great patron and guardian of our persons, liberties, and properties, and whatsoever is justly precious to us', declared petitioners from Suffolk. '... The only probable means under God left us, for the securing the rights, freedoms, peace and safety, and the effecting the settlement of this nation', pronounced petitioners from Cornwall. Without it, 'the undoubted birthright of the English nation, in their persons, estates, and all liberties, both religious and civil, can never be preserved ...', said London householders. Apprentices and young men of London avowed:

> That the glory of our nation, and the greatest comfort of our lives in our civil interests, consists in the privileges and liberties to which we were born, and which are the undoubted inherit- ance of all the free people of England, among which the grand and essential privilege which discriminates free men from slaves, is the interest which every man has in the legislative power of the nation, by their representatives assembled in parliament; without which, however we may flatter ourselves, or be flattered by others, we are truly no better than vassals governed by the will and pleasure of those who have no relation to us or our common interests.

Warwickshire petitioners believed that 'our rights and liberties, and privileges of parliament' were the 'Good Old Cause'; and Buckinghamshire petitioners concluded that the cry for a 'free parliament' was 'the voice of the whole people, and that is the voice of God ...'.

It was insisted upon in petition after petition:

> We do claim and avow it to be our undoubted birthright and liberty, that no new laws, much less any new government, can, or ought to be imposed upon us; nor any taxes, contributions, or free-quarter taken of us without the consent of the people of this nation in a free parliament assembled ... .

That was from Gloucestershire, and this from Warwickshire:

> It being the indubitable and indisputable right of all the free- born people of England, that no tax or imposition whatsoever, be put upon, or exacted from them, but by their representatives in parliament.

Lincolnshire said that only 'a free full parliament ... wherein the votes of all the free people of this nation may be included ... can have a legal capacity to enact laws and statutes, that may equally bind all the free people of England ...'. '... According to the fun- damental laws and constitutions of this nation', insisted Gloucestershire, it is 'the undoubted birthright of all the free-born people of England, that no tax or other imposition be exacted from them, or any new law imposed upon them, but by their consents had by their representatives in a full and free parliament'.

It followed from the ideology of the campaign for a 'free parliament' that it would incite refusals to pay taxes. Londoners urged that no taxes be paid until there was a 'free parliament' (Davies 1955: 277–8). Declarations from Essex, Bedfordshire, Lincolnshire, Gloucestershire, Warwickshire, Yorkshire and the city of Westminster supported a campaign of tax refusal. It is not clear how far this was implemented but the threat alone was a significant reinforcement of the demands for a 'free parliament'.

Since republicans still controlled the levers of power and the army, it may have been prudent to avoid references to monarchy, but it is difficult to dismiss the language of these petitions as no more than a cloak over the true intentions of the petitioners to bring back a king. The primary aim was to have laws and taxes enacted by the consent of a 'full and free parliament', and if that led to the restoration of the monarchy, it was to be seen in terms of re-establishing parliamentary forms of government.

Counter-Revolution

General Monck persuaded the army to acquiesce in the reinstatement of the MPs who had been purged from parliament in December 1648, and then to parliament dissolving itself and calling new elections. The fact that this led to the restoration of the monarchy was due to two occurrences between February and April 1660: an upsurge of popular support for a king and the regaining of political power by the old ruling class.

In May 1659 Harrington had judged in a pamphlet *Pour enclouer le canon* that 'the far greater part' of the people favoured monarchy. Yet they did not often give expression to that opinion and had not so far appeared forward to act upon it. But popular support for a king did surface at the end of February 1660; for example, a crowd gathered in the market-place at Durham and 'some of the rabble began to cry for a king and a free parliament ...', and in Nottingham a 'crowd marched up and down with colours flying, crying out, "A King! A King!"' (HMC 1899: 159, 162). The unpopularity of the republican regime arose at least in part from the heavy taxes for the support of a large army, and the popularity of the restoration of the monarchy from the expectation that it would get rid of the army and reduce the taxes. A fuller of Aby in Lincolnshire took a garland with which some children were playing and put it on the head of his companion, 'and said he therewith crowned him king, and he said he would put him into the power of princely government and waited at his stirrup bareheaded, and desired he would please to take off taxes and excise and other oppressions from the nation' (Holmes 1980: 219).

> It is hard to determine the exact grounds for the popular enthusiasm for the restored monarchy. Some of it at least may have stemmed from false expectations as to what its rule would actually bring. Before the Restoration, Marchamount Nedham had attributed popular royalism to a belief that Charles II's return would mean 'Peace and No Taxes'. On both counts the people would be rudely disillusioned. (Coleby 1987: 117, 142.)

The army and the republican ruling class began to disintegrate in the face of popular hostility. What fundamentally happened in 1660 was not so much that the monarchy was restored as that the peers and greater gentry – the old ruling class – rode to political power on the back of the campaign for a 'free parliament', and from February onwards regained control over the local militias and county governments, well before Charles II was recalled to the throne in May. (Davies 1955: 298; Hill 1984: 284–5; Hutton 1987: 103; 1990: 129; Morrill 1992: 110.)

CHAPTER 8

Conclusion: The Unfinished Revolution

... I would fain know what the soldier has fought for all this while?
He has fought to enslave himself, to give power to men of
riches, men of estates, to make him a perpetual slave.

COLONEL THOMAS RAINBOROUGH, 1647

The mass of the population still consisted of peasants and most of
them were not radicalised by the revolution. The regimes of the
1650s protected enclosures, indeed promoted them, and showed
no interest in a general enfranchisement of copyholders to give them
the security of tenure of freeholders. There were numerous riots
against enclosures in the forests and fens, and refusals to pay
increased rents and entry fines in many other places, but John Walter
is broadly right to say that most of the radicals 'failed to provide
either an effective programme or leadership for rural discontent'
(Walter 1991: 120–1). But Lilburne, the Leveller leader, did
belatedly involve himself directly in the long struggle of the Epworth
peasants (as noted in Chapter 4) to retain their commons (Lindley
1982: ch. 6). At Cobham, where there was a long history of conflict
between the peasants and the lord of the manor over the level of
rents and entry fines, and access to timber resources, the Diggers
(see Chapter 6: 116–17) did win some local support from landless
labourers and cottagers as well as from some of the 'middling
sort', showing that '... given the right local conditions, the radical
ideas which circulated during the later 1640s could find a receptive
audience in rural communities ...' (Gurney 1994).

Had radicals given leadership directly in the localities to dis-
contented peasants it is possible that a revolutionary agrarian
movement might have developed and destroyed the economic
power of the aristocracy, but it is probably unlikely in the existing
society and culture that they could have mobilised for revolution
any large sections of the smaller peasantry and rural poor. '... In
view of the ideological hegemony exercised by local landlords over
most of the countryside and the relative immunity of agricultural
labourers to radical politics in this epoch, relatively little mass
radicalisation could have been expected at this time from rural
England, except perhaps from the rural industrial districts, under
any conditions' (Brenner 1993: 539). The peasants generally,
under the influence of conservative clergy as well as landlords,

remained attached to the old constitution and the old church. Like the clubmen, as described in Chapter 5, they would stand for government by King, Lords and Commons, against arbitrary rule and high taxes whether imposed by crown or parliament, and for the church as established by Elizabeth I against 'papists' and 'sectaries'. It may be said that the clubmen of 1645 won a belated victory in 1660.

The republican ruling groups were unable to maintain themselves in political power in the face of popular discontent and aristocratic resurgence because they were losing their bases of support amongst the 'middle sort of people'. Repeated military coups and continuing threats of military intervention in politics created political instability which damaged trade. A main motive for the Restoration was to disband the army, and an important legacy of the revolution was fear of a standing army as a danger to liberty. In the 1640s crucial sections of the 'middle sort' had viewed the king and the aristocracy as threats to their religious beliefs and political freedom, and indeed to their prosperity and their standing in the community. In the 1650s they were coming to regard their own radical wing, as exemplified by the Levellers, in alliance with more plebeian elements, as the greater menace. In the 1640s they had feared 'papists', in the 1650s they feared 'sectaries' even more, as threats to order and stability.

The dilemma of the revolution was that the 'middle sort' wanted local autonomy, which acquired a comprehensive political programme with the Levellers, but this conflicted with their need for a strong central government equipped to keep the poor in their place and to make England a great power internationally, capable of aggressively promoting commerce and colonisation. They wanted control over their local church and its minister, but most of them did not desire to follow the radicals into demolishing the national church and its parish structure, especially as the latter sustained their local pre-eminence. They wanted a simpler, speedier, cheaper legal system, which would give them equality before the law and protect their rights and properties, but they were doubtful about the extent of decentralisation favoured by radicals. Local courts, without professional lawyers, presided over by elected judges and juries, would have been capable of dealing with many crimes and disputes, but incapable of coping with the problems of a society being shaped by the development of capitalism and involvement in national and international markets (Aylmer 1986: 126). The republican regimes of the 1650s went some way towards fashioning a strong, centralised state organised for naval, commercial and colonial power, and this was more satisfactory and profitable for leading sections of the 'middle sort of people' than the weak central government and strong local democracy advocated by the Levellers

(Brenner 1993: 714–15). Those interested in colonisation in Ireland and the West Indies were at the heart of the parliamentarian party (as noted in Chapter 4). A pointer to the future was Cromwell's seizure in 1655 of Jamaica, which became a base for the slave trade and illicit commerce with the Spanish colonies, generating the capital for sugar plantations. 'It is an historic turning-point: for the next 150 years the West Indies was crucial to English imperial and foreign policy' (Hill 1970: 158–61).

The fundamental fact is that the aristocracy was not expropriated by the revolution: it retained its estates and its status, though deprived temporarily of its political power. In essence the Restoration was the re-establishment of the aristocracy in political power, but under new terms of relationship to a state evolving into a great naval, commercial, colonial and industrial power, and to increasing interdependence with the 'middle sort of people'. The 'middle sort' could not prevent the resurgence of the aristocracy because they were divided into more conservative and more radical elements, the latter opposing but the former accepting alliance with the aristocracy in order to defeat radical demands. The 'middle sort' were also divided between elements rising to become capitalists and elements declining to become waged workers, and the former were willing to accept again the political hegemony of the aristocracy as a result of a growing convergence of economic interests. The aristocracy which re-emerged as the ruling class in 1660 was more closely tied to the growth of capitalist farming than before 1640, and landowners won from the revolution the abolition of feudal tenures and the Court of Wards, which, by giving them absolute ownership of their estates and relieving them of costs when the heir was a minor, facilitated investment of capital in agriculture. The bigger farmers were more closely linked to the larger landowners in the promotion of enclosures and agricultural 'improvements' than before 1640. But the 'middle sort' retained their distinctiveness from the aristocracy and their capacity for independent political action. (Wrightson 1982: 223–4, 226–8; Walter 1991: 120–2; Morrill 1992: 105–7; Brenner 1993: 711; Barry 1994: 201, 206–8; Hill 1980.)

'There is mounting evidence', observes Barry Coward, 'that the traditional view that the process of social change slowed down after 1650 needs revising ...'. Although small independent farmers survived and even prospered in pastoral areas, they were being eliminated in arable areas. In place of a two-tier social structure of landlords and peasants, as prevailed across Europe, the trend in England was towards a three-tier social structure of large landowners, capitalist farmers, and a mass of landless wage-earners (Coward 1988: 33, 51–3, 101). As capitalism advanced, more and more of the people lost possession of the land – the most important means of production in a pre-industrial society. Before and during the revolution great numbers of the landless had migrated to the uncultivated commons and wastes, notably in the forests, squatting in cottages and cabins and getting some sort of livelihood, or part of it, from the land. There was an urgent need felt by the established communities, especially by the 'middle sort', to turn back this tide of impoverished people. Soon after the Restoration the Act of Settlement was passed and this empowered JPs to expel newcomers from a parish and send them back to their place of origins. The reason given for this act was the 'poor people ... do endeavour to settle themselves in those parishes where there is the best stock, the largest commons or wastes to build cottages and the most woods for them to burn and destroy' (Hill 1969: 176–8).

Agriculture productivity increased, manufacturing developed and commerce expanded under the impetus of growing home and colonial markets. Urbanisation accelerated and non-landed elements in society grew in importance, 'drawn from middling groups, like craftsmen, merchants, artisans, manufacturers and professional people' – 'people who gained their living primarily from manufacturing, trade and the provision of professional and other services'. There emerged a state adapted to the accumulation of capital and the disciplining of labour, and to commercial and imperial expansion. This rested upon its achievement of legitimacy in the eyes of 'middling sort' as well as aristocrats. That came about from a new and unique combination of representative institutions (howsoever limited in scope) and checks on the power of the monarch (though still not irreversible) with a strong central government able to mobilise the nation's financial and military resources on a scale inconceivable in the first half of the seventeenth century, and so to achieve the status of a great power militarily and economically. (Coward 1988: 33, 51–3, 101; Innes 1987: 177–9, 195–7; Hill 1990: ch. 2.)

In two other respects the impact of the English Revolution proved irreversible after the Restoration. First, Cromwell's army resolved definitively the problems of England's relations with Scotland and Ireland. In the 1640s the Scots and the Irish had tried to pursue their own interests by exploiting the differences in England. But now they could no longer exert independent roles, and the hegemony of the English ruling class was fastened upon the entire archipelago, which, in the words of Ronald Hutton, 'has never recovered from its remoulding by the people who executed Charles I' (Hutton 1990: 135).

Second, the king had striven for religious uniformity in the 1630s and so had parliament in the 1640s. The bishops and liturgy of the Church of England (now properly termed the Anglican Church) were restored in 1660, but all the people could not be re-incorporated into a single national church. The religious sects had established themselves sufficiently during the revolution that they could not be eradicated by the renewed persecution thereafter. The long and bitter struggle in the revolution for religious toleration continued. A permanent fissure was opened in English society between Anglicans and Dissenters, which had profound influence on English political, cultural and educational life for the next three centuries (Hughes 1992b: 89–90; Fletcher 1990: 231–3). This was a turning-point in the history of England: the modern state developed, not on the unitary principle of the past, but on an evolving pluralistic principle, incorporating different traditions in religion and in politics, rival religions and rival political parties. The hegemony of the culture, which the Church of England had sustained in the interests of the monarchical state and its aristocratic ruling class, was no longer intact, and an alternative culture now existed and many of the 'middling sort' and also more plebeian elements attached themselves to it.

The revolution began and ended with successful popular demands for the meeting of parliament. One abiding popular theme of the period was belief in a parliamentary constitution and the need for consent to legislation and taxation. Although the Levellers raised the question of extending the right to vote in parliamentary elections, the unrepresentative character of parliaments seemed to have concerned the popular mind less than principle of the existence of parliaments in the constitution. This counteracts the tendency to see popular movements during the revolution as motivated largely by religion or basically by economic distress. Parliamentary government had yet to establish itself but the revolution embedded in the popular mind the conviction that parliaments guaranteed the liberties of free-born Englishmen, even though the reality was very different: only the people themselves could guarantee their own liberties.

Bibliography

* Books marked with asterisk provide introductory and background reading.

Adamson, J.S.A. (1987) 'The English Nobility and the Projected Settlement of 1647', *Historical Journal*, vol. XXX.

Adamson, J.S.A. (1990) 'The Baronial Context of the English Civil War', *Transactions of the Royal Historical Society*, fifth series, vol. 40.

Andriette, Eugene (1971) *Devon and Exeter in the Civil War*, Newton Abbot.

Appleby, J.O. (1978) *Economic Thought and Ideology in Seventeenth-Century England*, Princeton.

Aylmer, G.E. (1972) 'Who was ruling in Herefordshire from 1645 to 1661?', *Transactions of the Woolhope Club*, no. 40.

Aylmer, G.E. (1980) 'Crisis and Regrouping in the Political Elites: England from the 1630s to the 1660s', in J.G.A. Pocock (ed.) *Three British Revolutions: 1641, 1688, 1776*, Princeton.

*Aylmer, G.E. (1986) *Rebellion or Revolution? England 1640–1660*, Oxford.

Barnes, T.G. (1961) *Somerset 1625–1640: A County's Government during the 'Personal Rule'*, London.

Barry, Jonathan (1994) 'The Making of the Middle Class?' *Past & Present*, no. 145.

Bell, Robert (1849) (ed.) *Memorial of the Civil War: The Fairfax Correspondence*, 2 vols, London.

Blackwood, B.G. (1978) *The Lancashire Gentry and the Great Rebellion 1640–60*, Manchester.

Blackwood, B.G. (1993) 'Parties and Issues in the Civil War in Lancashire and East Anglia', *Northern History*, vol. XXIX.

Braddick, Michael (1991) 'Popular Politics and Public Policy: The Excise Riot at Smithfield in February 1647 and its Aftermath', *Historical Journal*, vol. XXXIV.

Brailsford, H.N. (1961) *The Levellers and the English Revolution*, London.

Brenner, Robert (1993) *Merchants and Revolution: Commercial Change, Political Conflict and London's Overseas Traders, 1550–1653*, Cambridge.

Campbell, Mildred (1960) *The English Yeoman under Elizabeth and the Early Stuarts*, London.

Capp, B.S. (1972) *The Fifth Monarchy Men*, London.

Carlin, Norah (1980–81) 'Marxism and the English Civil War', *International Socialism*, no. 10.

Carlin, Norah (1994) 'Liberty and Fraternities in the English Revolution: The Politics of London Artisans' Protests, 1635–1659', *International Review of Social History*, no. 39.

Carlton, Charles (1994) *Going to the Wars: The Experience of the British Civil Wars 1638–1651*, London.

Clark, Peter (1977) *English Provincial Society from the Reformation to the Revolution: Religion, Politics and Society in Kent 1500–1640*, Hassocks.

Cliffe, J.T. (1969) *The Yorkshire Gentry from the Reformation to the Civil War*, London.

Cliffe, J.T. (1988) *Puritans in Conflict: The Puritan Gentry During and After the Civil Wars*, London.

Coleby, Andrew (1987) *Central Government and the Localities: Hampshire 1649–1689*, Cambridge.

*Coward, Barry (1988) *Social Change and Continuity in Early Modern England 1550–1750*, London.

CSPD *Calendar of State Papers Domestic*.

Davies, Godfrey (1955) *The Restoration of Charles II 1658–1660*, San Marino.

Dobb, Maurice (1946) *Studies in the Development of Capitalism*, London.

Elliott, J.H. (1970) 'Revolts in the Spanish Monarchy', in Robert Forster and Jack P. Greene (eds) *Preconditions of Revolution in Early Modern Europe*, Baltimore.

Evans, John T. (1979) *Seventeenth-Century Norwich: Politics, Religion, and Government, 1620–1690*, Oxford.

Everitt, Alan (1960) *Suffolk and the Great Rebellion*, Suffolk Records Society, vol. III.

Everitt, Alan (1966) *The Community of Kent and the Great Rebellion 1640–60*, Leicester.

Firth, C.H. (1910) *The House of Lords during the Civil War*, London.

Firth, C.H. and Davies, Godfrey (1940) *The Regimental History of Cromwell's Army*, two vols, Oxford.

Fissel, M.C. (1994) *The Bishops' Wars: Charles I's Campaigns against Scotland, 1638–1640*, Cambridge.

Fletcher, Anthony (1975) *A County Community in Peace and War: Sussex 1600–1660*, London.

Fletcher, Anthony (1981) *The Outbreak of the English Civil War*, London.

Fletcher, Anthony (1990) 'Oliver Cromwell and the Godly Nation', in John Morrill (ed.) *Oliver Cromwell and the English Revolution*, Harlow.

Gardiner, S.R. (1893) *History of the Great Civil War 1642–1649*, four vols, London.

Gardiner, S.R. (1899) *History of England 1603–1642*, ten vols, London.

Gardiner, S.R. (1906) *The Constitutional Documents of the Puritan Revolution 1625–1660*, Oxford.

Gentles, Ian (1992) *The New Model Army in England, Ireland and Scotland, 1645–1653*, Oxford.

Gladwish, Paul (1985) 'The Herefordshire Clubmen', *Midland History*, vol. X.

Green, I.M. (1979) 'The Persecution of "Scandalous" and "Malignant" Parish Clergy during the English Civil War', *English Historical Review*, vol. 94.

Gurney, John (1994) 'Gerard Winstanley and the Digger Movement in Walton and Cobham', *Historical Journal*, vol. XXXVII.

Harris, Tim (1987) *London Crowds in the Reign of Charles II*, Cambridge.

Herrup, Cynthia (1988) 'The Counties and the Country', in Geoff Eley and William Hunt (eds) *Reviving the English Revolution*, London.

Higgins, Patricia (1973) 'The Reactions of Women', in Brian Manning (ed.) *Politics, Religion and the English Civil War*, London.

Hill, Christopher (1956) *Economic Problems of the Church from Archbishop Whitgift to the Long Parliament*, Oxford.

Hill, Christopher (1964) *Society and Puritanism in Pre-Revolutionary England*, London.

*Hill, Christopher (1969) *Reformation to Industrial Revolution*, Harmondsworth.

Hill, Christopher (1970) *God's Englishman: Oliver Cromwell and the English Revolution*, London.

Hill, Christopher (1980) 'A Bourgeois Revolution?', in J.G.A. Pocock (ed.) *Three British Revolutions: 1641, 1688, 1776*, Princeton.

Hill, Christopher (1984) *The Experience of Defeat: Milton and Some Contemporaries*, London.

Hill, Christopher (1990) *A Nation of Change and Novelty: Radical Politics, Religion and Literature in Seventeenth-Century England*, London.

Hill, Christopher (1993) *The English Bible and the Seventeenth-Century Revolution*, Harmondsworth.

Hilton, Rodney (1976) (ed.) *The Transition from Feudalism to Capitalism*, London.

HMC (1888): *Historical Manuscripts Commission*, Cowper (Coke) Mss, vol. II.

HMC (1894): *Historical Manuscripts Commission*, Portland Mss, vol. III.

HMC (1899): *Historical Manuscripts Commission*. Leyborne-Popham Mss.

Hobbes, Thomas (1969) *Behemoth, or the Long Parliament*, ed. Ferdinand Tonnies, 2nd edn, London.

Hodgson, John (1806) 'Memoirs of Captain John Hodgson', in *Original Memoirs Written During the Great Civil War*, Edinburgh.

Holmes, Clive (1974) *The Eastern Association in the English Civil War*, Cambridge.

Holmes, Clive (1980) *Seventeenth-Century Lincolnshire*, Lincoln.

Howell, Roger (1967) *Newcastle upon Tyne and the Puritan Revolution*, Oxford.

Hughes, Ann (1987) *Politics, Society and Civil War in Warwickshire, 1620–1660*, Cambridge.

Hughes, Ann (1989) 'Local History and the Origins of the Civil War', in Richard Cust and Ann Hughes (eds) *Conflict in Early Stuart England: Studies in Religion and Politics 1603–1642*, London.

*Hughes, Ann (1991) *The Causes of the English Civil War*, London.

Hughes, Ann (1992a) 'Coventry and the English Revolution', in R.C. Richardson (ed.) *Town and Countryside in the English Revolution*, Manchester.

Hughes, Ann (1992b) 'The Frustration of the Godly', in John Morrill (ed.) *Revolution and Restoration in England in the 1650s*, London.

Hunt, William (1983) *The Puritan Moment: The Coming of Revolution in an English County*, Cambridge, Mass.

Hutchinson, Lucy (1885) *Memoirs of the Life of Colonel Hutchinson*, ed. C.H. Firth, two vols, London.

Hutton, Ronald (1982) *The Royalist War Effort 1642–1646*, London.

Hutton, Ronald (1987) *The Restoration: A Political and Religious History of England and Wales 1658–1667*, Oxford.

Hutton, Ronald (1990) *The British Republic 1649–1660*, London.

Innes, Joanna (1987) 'Jonathan Clark, Social History and England's "Ancien Regime"', *Past & Present*, no. 115.

Johnson, G.W. (1848) (ed.) *Memoirs of the Reign of Charles I: The Fairfax Correspondence*, two vols, London.

Josselin, Ralph (1976) *Diary*, ed. Alan Macfarlane, Oxford.

Kishlansky, Mark (1979) *The Rise of the New Model Army*, Cambridge.

Levine, David and Wrightson, Keith (1991) *The Making of an Industrial Society: Whickham 1560–1765*, Oxford.

Lindley, Keith (1982) *Fenland Riots and the English Revolution*, London.

Lindley, Keith (1992) 'London's Citizenry in the English Revolution', in R.C. Richardson (ed.) *Town and Countryside in the English Revolution*, Manchester.

Lindley, Keith (1994) 'Irish Adventurers and Godly Militants in the 1640's, *Irish Historical Studies*, vol. XXIX.

Ludlow, Edmund (1894) *Memoirs*, ed. C.H. Firth, two vols, Oxford.

McGregor, J.F. and Reay, Barry (1984) (eds) *Radical Religion in the English Revolution*, Oxford.

Malcolm, Joyce (1983) *Caesar's Due: Loyalty and King Charles 1642–1646*, London.

Manning, Brian (1973) 'The Aristocracy and the Downfall of Charles I', in Brian Manning (ed.) *Politics, Religion and the English Civil War*, London.

Manning, Brian (1991) *The English People and the English Revolution*, new edn, London.

Manning, Brian (1992) *1649: The Crisis of the English Revolution*, London.

Massarella, Derek (1981) 'The Politics of the Army and the Quest for Settlement', in Ivan Roots (ed.) *'Into Another Mould': Aspects of the Interregnum*, Exeter.

Morrill, John (1974) *Cheshire 1630–1660: County Government and Society during the English Revolution*, Oxford.

Morrill, John (1976) *The Revolt of the Provinces: Conservatives and Radicals in the English Civil War, 1630–1650*, London.

Morrill, John (1982) (ed.) *Reactions to the English Civil War 1642–1649*, London.

Morrill, John (1992) (ed.) *Revolution and Restoration in England in the 1650s*, London.

Morrill, John (1993) *The Nature of the English Revolution*, London.

O'Riordan, Christopher (1993) 'Popular Exploitation of Enemy Estates in the English Revolution', *History*, vol. 78.

Pam, D.O. (1977) 'The Rude Multitude: Enfield and the Civil War', *Edmonton Hundred Historical Society*, Occasional Paper (New Series), no. 33.

Pearl, Valerie (1961) *London and the Outbreak of the Puritan Revolution*, Oxford.

Pearl, Valerie (1972) 'London's Counter-Revolution', in G.E. Aylmer (ed.) *The Interregnum: The Quest for Settlement 1646–1660*, London.

Peck, Francis (1732–35) *Desiderata Curiosa*, two vols, London.

Priestley, Jonathan (1883) 'Some memoirs concerning the family of the Priestleys', *Surtees Society*, vol. LXXVII.

Reay, Barry (1985) *The Quakers and the English Revolution*, New York.

Roberts, Stephen (1985) *Recovery and Restoration in an English County: Devon Local Administration 1646–1670*, Exeter.

Roberts, Stephen (1986) 'Godliness and Government in Glamorgan, 1647–1660', in Colin Jones, Malyn Newitt and Stephen Roberts (eds) *Politics and People in Revolutionary England*, Oxford.

Rollison, David (1992) *The Local Origins of Modern Society: Gloucestershire 1500–1800*, London.

Russell, Conrad (1987) 'The British Problem and the English Civil War', *History*, vol. 72.

Russell, Conrad (1991) *The Fall of the British Monarchies 1637–1642*, Oxford.

Sacks, David (1992) 'Bristol's Wars of Religion', in R.C. Richardson (ed.) *Town and Countryside in the English Revolution*, Manchester.

Sharp, Buchanan (1980) *In Contempt of All Authority: Rural Artisans and Riot in the West of England, 1586–1660*, Berkeley.

Sharp, Buchanan (1985) 'Popular Protest in Seventeenth-Century England', in Barry Reay (ed.) *Popular Culture in Seventeenth-Century England*, London.

Sharp, Buchanan (1988) 'Common Rights, Charities and the Disorderly Poor', in Geoff Eley and William Hunt (eds) *Reviving the English Revolution*, London.

Sharp, Buchanan (1992) 'Rural Discontent and the English Revolution', in R.C. Richardson (ed.) *Town and Countryside in the English Revolution*, Manchester.

Sharpe, Jim (1986) 'Scandalous and Malignant Priests in Essex: The Impact of Grassroots Puritanism', in Colin Jones, Malyn Newitt and Stephen Roberts (eds) *Politics and People in Revolutionary England*, Oxford.

Sharpe, Kevin (1992) *The Personal Rule of Charles I*, New Haven.

Skipp, Victor (1978) *Crisis and Development: An Ecological Study of the Forest of Arden 1570–1674*, Cambridge.

Smith, Alan G.R. (1984) *The Emergence of a Nation State: The Commonwealth of England 1529–1660*, London.

Smith, David L. (1992) 'Catholic, Anglican or Puritan? Edward Sackville, Fourth Earl of Dorset and the Ambiguities of Religion in Early Stuart England', *Transactions of the Royal Historical Society*, sixth series, vol. II.

Smith, David L. (1994) *Constitutional Royalism and the Search for Settlement, c 1640–1649*, Cambridge.

Smith, Steven R. (1978–79) 'Almost Revolutionaries: The London Apprentices during the Civil War', *Huntington Library Quarterly*, vol. XLII.

SPClar: *State Papers Collected by Edward, Earl of Clarendon*, two vols, Oxford.

Stoyle, Mark (1994) *Loyalty and Locality: Popular Allegiance in Devon during the English Civil War*, Exeter.

Sylvester, Matthew (1696) (ed.) *Reliquiae Baxterianae*, London.

Taft, Barbara (1985) 'The Council of Officers' "Agreement of the People", 1648–9', *Historical Journal*, vol. XXVII.

Tolmie, Murray (1977) *The Triumph of the Saints: The Separate Churches of London 1616–1649*, Cambridge.

Tyacke, Nicholas (1987) *Anti-Calvinists: The Rise of English Arminianism c 1590–1640*, Oxford.

Underdown, David (1971) *Pride's Purge: Politics in the Puritan Revolution*, Oxford.

Underdown, David (1973) *Somerset in the Civil War and Interregnum*, Newton Abbot.

Underdown, David (1979) 'The Chalk and the Cheese: Contrasts among the English Clubmen', *Past & Present*, no. 85.

Underdown, David (1980) 'Community and Class: Theories of Local Politics', in Barbara C. Malement (ed.) *After the Reformation*, Manchester.

Underdown, David (1985) *Revel, Riot, and Rebellion: Popular Politics and Culture in England 1603–1660*, Oxford.

Walter, John (1991) 'The Impact on Society: A World Turned Upside Down?', in John Morrill (ed.) *The Impact of the English Civil War*, London.

Washbourn, J. (1823) *Bibliotheca Gloucestrensis*, two vols, Gloucester.

Wolfe, Don M. (1967) (ed.) *Leveller Manifestoes of the Puritan Revolution*, London.

Woodhouse, A.S.P. (1938) (ed.) *Puritanism and Liberty: Being the Army Debates (1647–9)*, London.

Woolrych, Austin (1980) 'Historical Introduction (1659–1660)', in Robert W. Ayers (ed.) *Complete Works of John Milton*, revised edn, vol. VII.

Woolrych, Austin (1987) *Soldiers and Statesmen: The General Council of the Army and its Debates, 1647–1648*, Oxford.

Wootton, David (1990) 'From Rebellion to Revolution: The Crisis of the Winter of 1642–3 and the Origins of Civil War Radicalism'. *English Historical Review*, vol. 105.

Wootton, David (1991) 'Leveller Democracy and the Puritan Revolution', in J.H. Burns and Mark Goldie (eds) *The Cambridge History of Political Thought 1450–1700*, Cambridge.

Wrightson, Keith (1982) *English Society 1580–1680*, London.

Wrightson, Keith (1991) 'Estates, Degrees and Sorts: Changing Perceptions of Society in Tudor and Stuart England', in Penelope J. Corfield (ed.) *Language, History and Class*, Oxford.

Wrightson, Keith and Levine, David (1979) *Poverty and Piety in an English Village: Terling, 1525–1700*, New York.

Wroughton, John (1992) *A Community at War: The Civil War in Bath and North Somerset 1642–1650*, Bath.

Index of Subjects

Index of Persons and Places